Picture Encyclopedia

Picture Encyclopedia

Steve Parker

Parragon

Bath • New York • Singapore • Hong Kong • Cologne • Delhi
Melbourne • Amsterdam • Johannesburg • Shenzhen

This edition published by Parragon Books Ltd in 2013
Parragon Books Ltd
Chartist House
15–17 Trim Street
Bath BA1 1HA, UK
www.parragon.com

Produced by Scintilla Editorial Limited, Chelmsford

ISBN 978-1-4454-6124-3
Printed in China

Contents

Introduction

How many bones do you have in your body? Which is the highest mountain? How do gears work? If you like asking questions like these, you are sure to enjoy this book.

The **Children's Picture Encyclopedia** is packed full of all kinds of interesting facts. You can read about the stars and space, and the world we live in. You can find out about animals and plants, and the amazing machines around us.

At the back of the book you will find a list of useful words with simple explanations. There is also a selection of helpful web sites where you can find more information on many of the topics covered in this book.

Our planet

Our home is called planet Earth. From far away in space, it looks like a huge blue ball. This is because seas and oceans cover nearly three-quarters of its surface. The land that can be seen appears green and brown. But often much of the Earth's surface is hidden by wispy white swirls. These are clouds. Beneath them lies the Earth we know, with its mountains, plains, valleys, rivers, and lakes.

Days and seasons

The ground we stand on seems still, but it is actually moving all the time. The Earth spins around once every 24 hours. This gives us day and night. The Earth also travels right around the Sun, once every year. This gives us the seasons.

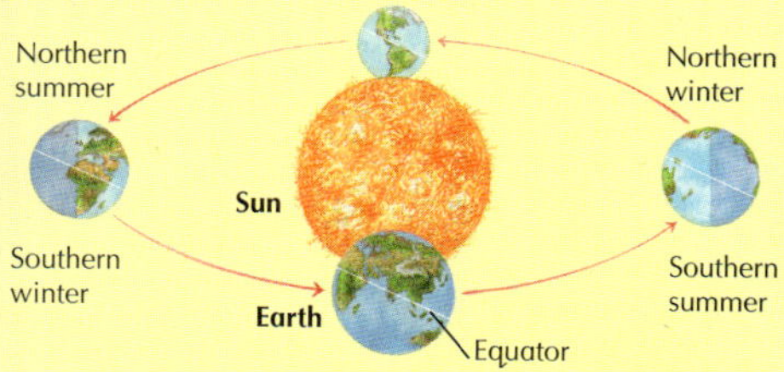

Seasonal journey

The Earth travels at more than 93,000 miles an hour in its journey around the Sun. As it flies through space it doesn't spin straight up, but is tilted at an angle. It is this tilt that gives the northern and southern parts of the Earth their summer and winter.

The seasons

We have spring and summer when our part of the Earth leans toward the Sun. We have fall and winter when our part of the Earth leans away from the Sun. The area around the middle of the Earth never tilts very much, so it is warm and sunny here most of the time.

Cold at the top and bottom

The top of the Earth is the North Pole. The bottom is the South Pole. These places are the polar regions. Here it is cold all year, with lots of ice and snow.

Sunrise, sunset

Every day the Sun seems to rise in the east, travel across the sky and set in the west. But it is really the Earth that is moving, not the Sun. Where the Earth turns to face the Sun it is daytime, and where it turns away from the Sun it is night.

Hot around the middle

Around the middle of the Earth lie the Tropics, where it is always hot. Some tropical places are dry deserts. Others are very wet, and are covered by rainforests.

Inside the Earth

Our Earth seems very hard and solid, and it is—but only on the outside. Inside, it is a mass of hot melted rock that slowly swirls around like honey being stirred.

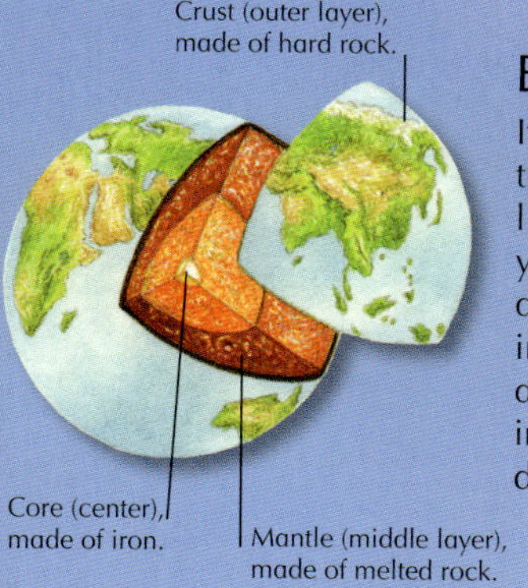

Earth layers

If you could cut the Earth open like a giant apple, you would see different layers inside. Just as an apple has a core in the middle, so does the Earth.

Hot jet

Sometimes water underground comes into contact with hot rocks inside the Earth. This makes the water heat up. The water may flow out on the surface as a hot spring. Sometimes the water gets so hot it boils and shoots out of the ground as a jet of steam and spray; this is called a geyser.

Hot springs

Some countries have a lot of hot springs, and people use the water for baths and to heat their homes. In Japan, monkeys called macaques have discovered that bathing in these springs is a great way to stay warm in winter!

Drilling holes

We dig mines to find coal, metal, and precious jewels. We drill holes to find oil and gas, and to study the Earth. Some holes go down more than 6 miles deep. It would take you three hours to reach the bottom in an elevator.

Different rocks

As we dig into the ground, we see many different layers of soil and rocks. The deeper we dig, the older the rocks get. Some formed many millions of years ago.

Volcanoes and earthquakes

The loudest explosions are made by volcanoes. They blast out smoke, ash, and red-hot rocks. Earthquakes are not as noisy, but they can make the land shake so much that the ground cracks and houses fall down.

Erupting volcano

When a volcano blows up, or erupts, it may make a terrible noise. Smoke rises high. Pieces of rock shoot out, some as big as houses! Red-hot melted rock, called lava, pours out, too. As the lava cools, it hardens.

Deep under the ground

A volcano forms where hot liquid rock bursts up through a crack or hole in the Earth's surface. Sometimes the lava just pours out of the volcano and flows down its sides. But if the lava gets blocked, the volcano may explode in a huge cloud of dust and ash.

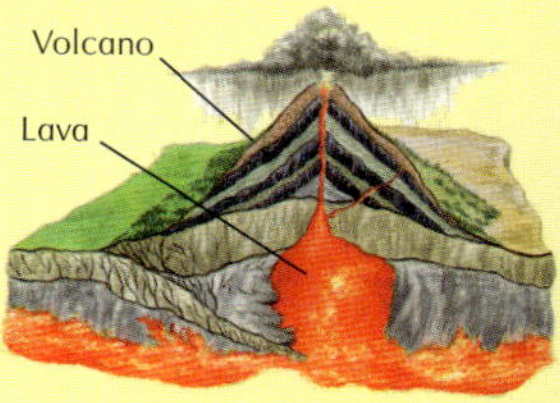

Giant wave

Sometimes an earthquake at the bottom of the sea pushes up the water into a huge wave. When the wave crashes onto the shore, it can destroy whole towns. The giant wave is called a tsunami.

Earth shaker

An earthquake makes the ground wobble and shake. Buildings and bridges fall down, roads crack open, and rail tracks bend. Electricity wires, gas pipes, and water pipes break. There is a great danger of electric shock, fires, and floods.

DID YOU KNOW?

If a volcano "goes to sleep" and is inactive for many years, it is called a dormant volcano. But it may "wake up" and explode at any time!

Weather

Will it be hot, cold, windy, or wet today? People like to know what the weather is going to be like, so they can plan their day. But for pilots and sailors, a weather forecast is even more important, since bad weather can be dangerous.

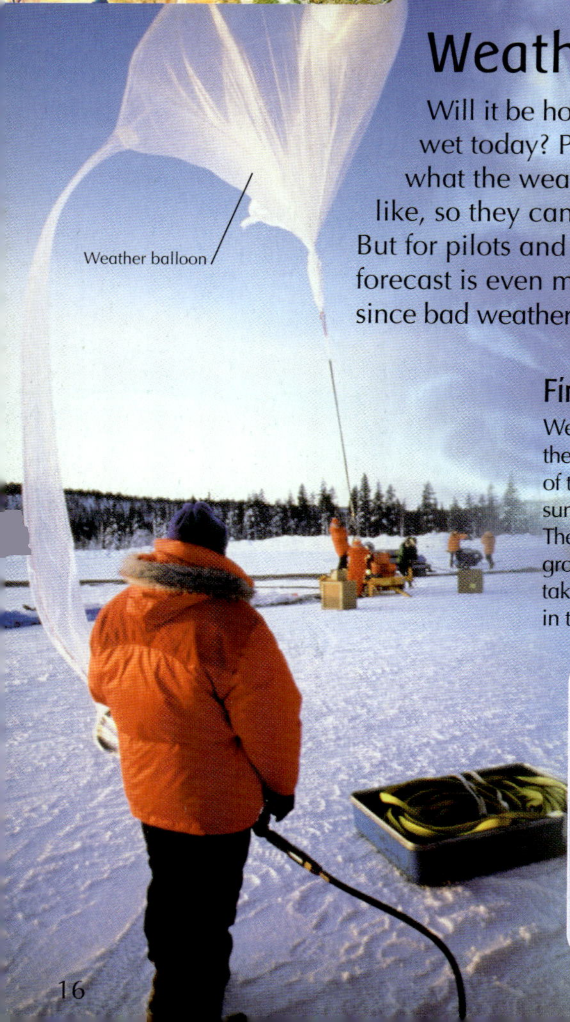

Finding out

Weather experts measure the temperature, the speed of the wind, and how much sunshine and cloud there is. They use instruments on the ground and balloons that take measurements high in the sky.

DID YOU KNOW?

As you go higher into the sky, the air gets much colder. People in an airplane are warm and comfortable, but outside the plane it is colder than a kitchen freezer!

Rain, hail, and snow

Clouds are made up of tiny water droplets. When the droplets fall to the ground, we call it rain. If it is cold and the water drops freeze into balls of ice, it is hail. When they freeze into ice crystals, they are called snow.

Clues from clouds

We can often tell what the weather is about to do from the shapes and colors of clouds. If they are very high and thin, it will probably be fine and sunny. Low, dark clouds usually bring rain.

Blowing

When air moves gently along we describe it as a breeze. When it blows very fast, it is a gale. If it gets any windier than a gale, it is called a storm or a hurricane. Winds this strong often blow trees over and cause damage to houses.

Storms and floods

A big storm can be frightening. The wind howls, lightning flashes, thunder booms, and the rain pours down. Some places have storms like this every few weeks.

Spinning wind

A tornado is a small, fast-moving column of spiraling wind. It is wide at the top and narrow at the bottom. Inside the tornado, the wind often moves almost as fast as a plane.

DID YOU KNOW?

Some tornadoes are so powerful that they pick up bicycles and even cars. Objects are sucked up high inside the tornado, before being thrown out at the top and sent crashing to the ground.

Thunder and lightning

A thundercloud is very tall, with a wide, dark base. Lightning is a giant spark of electricity, made when winds cause hail and water droplets in the cloud to bump together. The spark makes the air so hot that it explodes. This is the sound of thunder.

Seen from space

High in space, weather satellites look down on the Earth. They take pictures of the clouds and weather below. The swirling cloud in this picture is a violent tropical storm called a hurricane.

Too much rain

Some storms bring too much rain. If all the water can't flow away down drainpipes and along streams, it will flood the streets. Cars can be washed away and homes can be badly damaged.

Mountains and valleys

The highest places in the world are the tops of mountains. Between them are low, deep valleys. Mountain slopes can be very steep. Sometimes rocks and boulders come tumbling and crashing down. This is called a landslide.

Low down

Most valleys have a river along the bottom. The flowing water gradually cuts away the river bed and makes the valley deeper. Some valleys have steep sides and are called canyons or gorges.

Deep, dark caves

Sometimes a river flows down a crack in the ground. Over thousands of years, it wears away the rock and makes a big cave. Some caves are so big they could swallow up the largest football stadium with room to spare.

Shrinking mountains

Most mountains are millions of years old. But every year the wind, rain, and ice slowly wear the rocks away. Tiny pieces slither and slide down the valley sides, where they are swept away by rivers. Slowly the mountain becomes smaller.

On top of the world

The tops of mountains are usually cold and windy, and covered by ice and snow. They are often hidden in clouds. The highest mountain in the world is Mount Everest in the Himalayas. It is nearly 30,000 feet tall—17 times taller than the highest skyscraper.

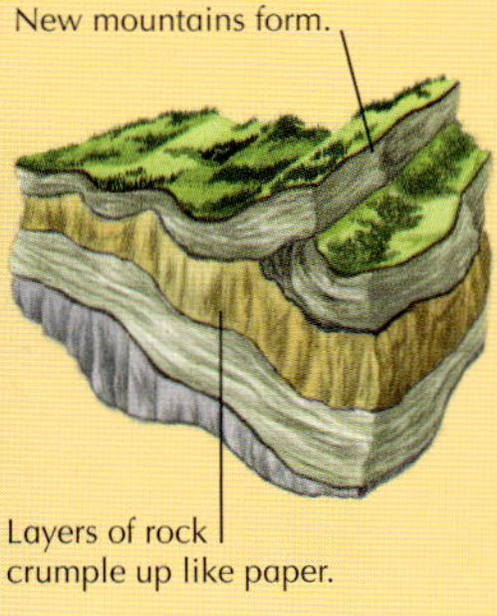

Making mountains

The Earth's crust is made up of lots of rocky plates that fit together like pieces of a jigsaw puzzle. These plates move slowly over the Earth's surface. If they bump into each other, the rocks can crumple together and push up new mountains.

Grasslands and deserts

Forests grow in places where there is plenty of rain. If there is less rain, grasses are the main plants. Where there is almost no rain, sandy or rocky deserts can form.

No rain left

Deserts often form near mountains. The rain falls on high ground as moist air rises up one side of the mountain. There is little or no rain left for the lowlands on the other side, which turn into desert.

Endless grass

Grasslands are wide and open, with just a few trees. The grass provides food for many different animals. The grasslands of Africa are called the savanna, and they are home to elephants, zebra, and wildebeest.

Seas of sand

Some deserts are rocky, with boulders and stones. Other deserts are sandy. The wind blows the sand into tall piles called dunes, which look a little like the waves on the ocean. It is very difficult to travel over the soft sand.

DID YOU KNOW?

The world's biggest desert is the Sahara Desert in North Africa. But the driest is the Atacama Desert in South America. In some parts of the Atacama, it hasn't rained at all for a hundred years!

Plant survivors

Most deserts get very little rain, and only a few tough plants are able to grow there. Many desert plants have sharp thorns, or spines, to stop animals from eating them. A cactus stores water in its wide, thick stem.

Woods and forests

A wood is a place with lots of trees and bushes. A forest is similar, but bigger. Woods and forests have lots of wildlife. Trees are home to many different animals.

Mixed woods

Places with mild weather often have mixed woodlands of many different kinds of tree. You can tell the trees apart by their leaves, fruit, and bark. Lots of animals, such as bears and deer, live in mixed woods.

Cold forests

In the far north, it is cold and snowy for half the year. The most common trees here are conifers. They have needle-like leaves and often have branches that slope down, so the snow falls off easily. Animals such as caribou, wolves, and bears take shelter among the trees.

Tropical forests

Tropical rainforests grow in places where it is always warm and wet. Many rainforest animals spend all their time in the trees. Orangutans hang by their long arms and swing through the branches. They feed on fruit, leaves, bark, and some insects.

Wildfires

In very dry weather a forest might catch fire. This could be caused by lightning or people being careless with matches! It can take up to a hundred years for the forest to grow again. But some plants have seeds that only grow after a forest fire.

Redwoods

The tallest trees in the world are coast redwoods. Some of these amazing trees measure more than 330 feet high, which is taller than 50 adults standing on top of each other.

Rivers and lakes

Where does all the rain go? It flows as water through ditches and drainpipes, and into streams and rivers. These may carry the water to ponds or lakes, or all the way to open water.

Life of a river

A river begins where many small streams come together. It then begins a long and winding journey that usually ends at the ocean.

Rushing rivers

Rivers high up in the hills usually rush and gush over rocks. Some rivers have waterfalls. The water pours over a cliff, formed by very hard rocks, and splashes into a deep pool underneath.

Water life

Rivers and lakes are often full of life. There are water birds, fish, frogs, snails, worms, and insects such as diving beetles. Most of these creatures live among reeds, rushes, waterlilies, and other plants.

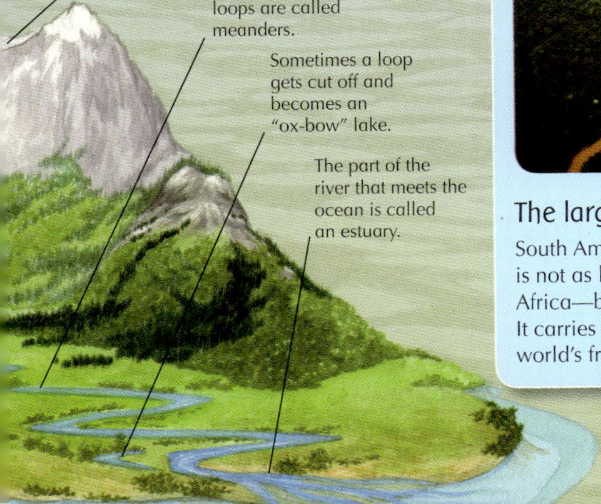

The largest river

South America's Amazon river is not as long as the Nile in Africa—but it is far bigger. It carries one-fifth of all the world's fresh water.

Waves and seashores

The edge of the land where it meets the ocean is called the coast, or shore. Many kinds of plants and animals live here, and people often visit the beach for their vacation.

Rocky shores

Some coasts are rocky. Rain, wind, and crashing waves slowly wear away the rocks. Sometimes the rocks are worn into strange shapes, such as arches, and tall columns called stacks.

Sandy shores

Some coasts are sandy, with wide, flat beaches. On sunny days people go to the beach to play, swim, sail boats, ride jet skis, and surf. Most people do not realize that many animals live in the sand, including worms and shellfish.

Up and down

Twice each day, the ocean rises at high tide and then falls at low tide. The difference in height between high tide and low tide can be as little as 3 feet, but in Canada's Bay of Fundy it is up to 55 feet.

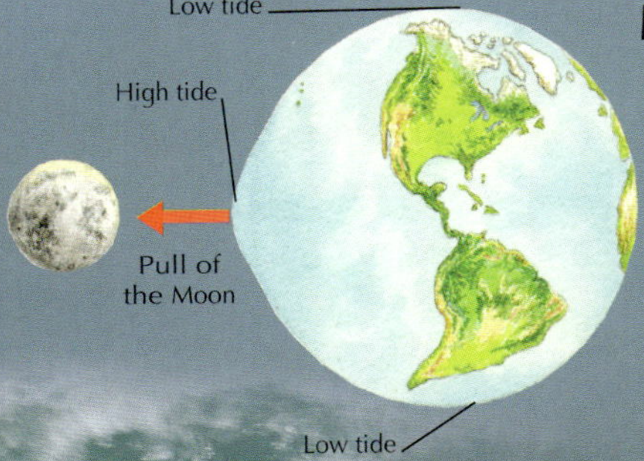

Moon's gravity

Tides are caused by the Moon's gravity, which pulls on the water in the seas and oceans as the Earth spins around. This makes the oceans bulge up in a high tide and causes other coasts to have low tide.

Danger at the coast

Along some coasts, there are rocks just under the water. Ships and boats must take care not to crash into them. A lighthouse warns of the danger.

DID YOU KNOW?

In some places the coast is made of very soft rock. The waves wear it away so that houses and even whole towns will gradually fall into the ocean.

Seas and oceans

Almost three-quarters of planet Earth is covered by seas and oceans. This is why the Earth looks so blue when seen from space.

Coral reefs

Where the water is warm, clear, and shallow, coral reefs may form. Tiny coral creatures make little cups of stone around their soft bodies. When they die, more coral creatures do the same on top. Gradually the reef grows. Reefs also attract hundreds of colorful fish.

DID YOU KNOW?

The deepest place on Earth is the Mariana Trench in the Pacific Ocean near Japan. It goes down nearly 7 miles. The tallest mountain would easily fit into it and still be underwater.

Silver shoals

Thousands of fish and other creatures live in the ocean. Some live around the shores. Others live out in the open water. Large groups of fish are called shoals.

New islands

Beneath the waves, the seabed is a lot like dry land. There are mountains and valleys, deep caves, and even volcanoes. Some undersea volcanoes grow so big that they break the surface and become islands.

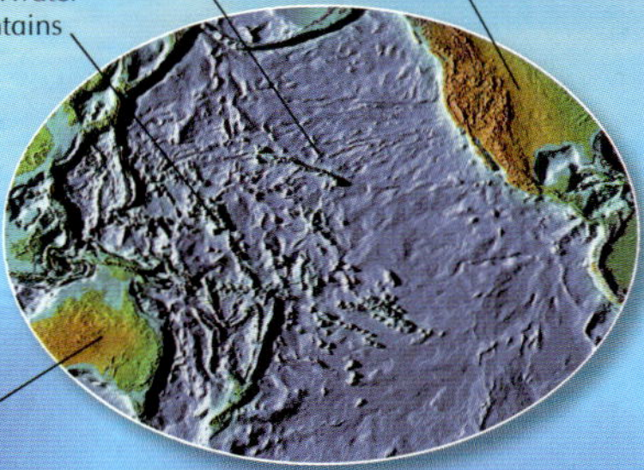

Under the waves

To explore the ocean depths, you need a submarine. This is because the deeper you go, the darker and colder it gets. The weight of all the water above also makes it difficult to move around.

Earth in trouble

The Earth is rich in useful resources, from coal and oil to many kinds of metal. It also provides us with water to drink and air to breathe. But we are using these resources up fast, and human activities are even changing the Earth's climate.

Melting glaciers

Frozen rivers, called glaciers, are beginning to melt because the Earth's temperature is slowly rising. This extra water will make the oceans rise higher and cause flooding.

Digging up land

We dig up coal from deep mines underground and open mines on the surface. Some open mines are bigger than 100 football fields. All this digging destroys the landscape and the homes of wild animals and plants.

Saving water

A lot of the water we drink comes from rain, but we also use water from underground lakes and wells that have taken thousands of years to fill up. Some of these wells have already run dry.

Why the Earth is getting warmer

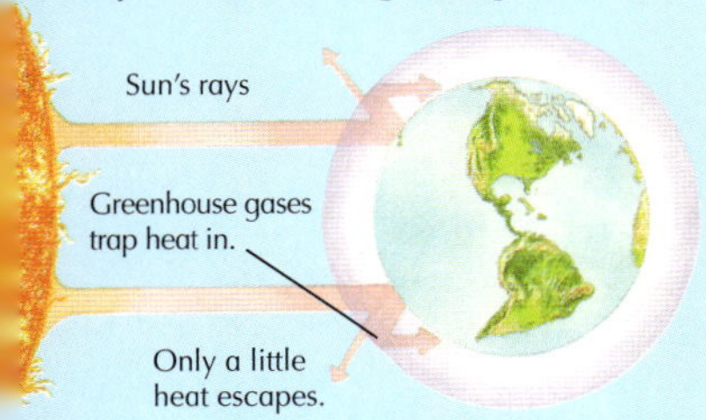

Recently scientists have noticed that the Earth is getting warmer. They think this is being caused by "greenhouse gases." These gases, such as the carbon dioxide we make when we burn oil and coal, act like the glass of a greenhouse, keeping the Sun's heat in and making the Earth warmer.

Using oil

These "nodding donkey" pumps bring oil to the surface from deep below ground. We use oil as fuel for our cars, and to make plastics, paints, and thousands of other useful things. But if we are not careful, we will soon use it all up.

From past to present

Historians and archaeologists are like detectives. They study the remains of ancient buildings, documents, tools, weapons—and even the bones of people and their animals. From all these clues they can build up a picture of what life must have been like a long time ago. They can also learn how the ideas and inventions from the past have helped form the world we live in today.

Long, long ago

When our planet Earth began, there was no life. Huge storms with lightning, thunder, and floods went on for millions of years. Rivers, lakes, and seas filled with water. Then came the first living things.

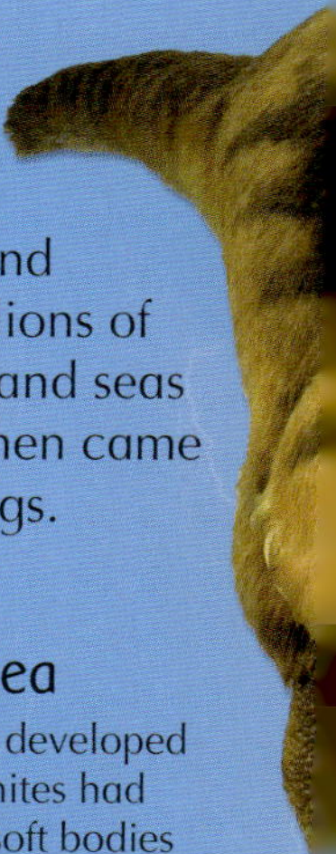

Ammonite fossil

Life begins at sea

The first living things developed in the ocean. Ammonites had snail-like shells and soft bodies that looked like miniature squid. They searched in the mud of the ocean floor for food scraps.

Life moves onto land

About 380 million years ago, some ocean creatures began to wriggle onto the shore. Over millions of years, some of them changed and were able to walk and breathe air. Others, including the horseshoe crab, have hardly changed at all.

Horseshoe crab

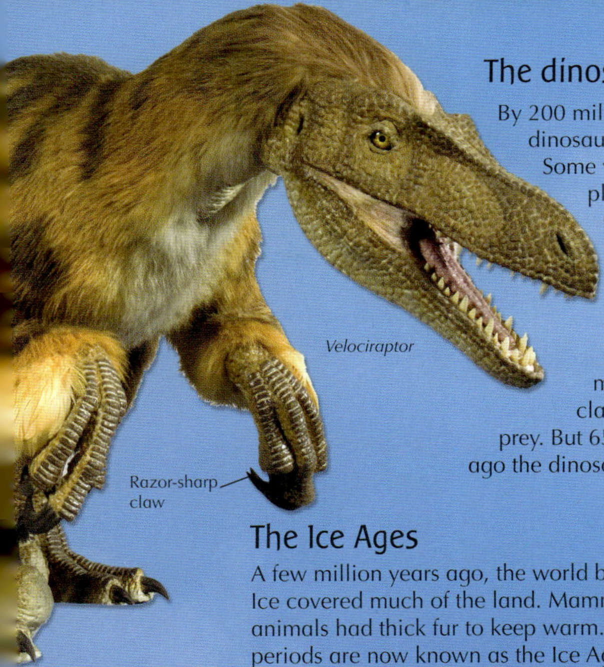

The dinosaurs

By 200 million years ago, dinosaurs ruled the land. Some were giant plant-eaters. Others were the biggest, fiercest hunters ever to walk the Earth. One of these, *Velociraptor*, had massive hooked claws to catch its prey. But 65 million years ago the dinosaurs died out.

The Ice Ages

A few million years ago, the world became colder. Ice covered much of the land. Mammoths and other animals had thick fur to keep warm. These cold periods are now known as the Ice Ages.

DID YOU KNOW?

We find out about animals from long ago by studying their fossils. These are the remains of bones and shells that became buried and turned to stone.

The first people

The first people gathered fruit and berries for food, and hunted wild animals. They moved around a lot, never staying anywhere for very long. Then about 10,000 years ago they started to settle down in villages. They built huts, planted crops, and kept farm animals.

Cave paintings

About 30,000 years ago, people painted wonderful pictures on the walls of dark caves. The pictures showed animals such as deer, buffalo, long-horned cattle, and horses.

Early people

The Neanderthal people were a lot like us. They used fire and made tools and clothes. They even painted pictures on the walls of caves. But they died out around 25,000 years ago.

Keeping animals

From about 10,000 years ago, people began keeping goats and sheep. Wild dogs were also tamed so that they could help people look after their animals.

Flint axe

Stone tools

Long before people discovered metal they made tools from wood, bone, and stone. A stone called flint was made into very sharp tools such as axes, knives, and arrowheads.

From caves to huts

Caves provided people with their first homes. But when people started living together in larger groups, they began to build their own homes from wood, leaves, stones, and mud.

The ancient world

The first great towns and cities were built in the Middle East and North Africa. The people who lived there invented writing and the wheel. They built temples for their gods and goddesses, and sent great armies to attack their enemies.

Pyramid builders

The ancient Egyptians lived along the River Nile in North Africa. They began to build their great stone mountains, called pyramids, about 4,600 years ago. The pyramids were tombs for the Egyptian kings, who were called pharaohs.

Trading by sea

From about 4,500 years ago, people called the Phoenicians lived on the shores of the Mediterranean. They traveled around the Mediterranean Sea in large sailing ships, buying and selling valuable goods such as wine and spices, glass, gold, and jewels.

Talented Greeks

Ancient Greece was very powerful 2,500 years ago. The Greeks were not only great warriors, but also skilled in art, science, and writing. Their style of building is still admired and copied today.

The Parthenon in Athens is a Greek temple built for the goddess Athena.

DID YOU KNOW?

The Colosseum was a huge stadium in Rome that could hold 50,000 people. Ancient Romans used to go there to watch fighters called gladiators battle to the death.

A great empire

About 2,000 years ago, the Romans had the best army in the world. The army was very well organized, with groups of 100 men each led by commanders called centurions. The army won many battles and helped the Romans build a great empire.

The birth of faith

Although people have always believed in gods and spirits, many of the world's great religions began between 1,500 and 3,000 years ago. Christianity, Islam, Buddhism, Sikhism, and Judaism all began at this time.

Buddhism

Siddhartha Gautama was born in India about 2,500 years ago. He gave up his possessions and worked to help the poor. Later he became known as Buddha.

Judaism

Jews believe that they have a special relationship with God and that they are his chosen people. One of their biggest festivals is called Hanukkah, the festival of lights.

Christianity

Christianity began just over 2,000 years ago and today is the world's largest religion, with about two billion followers. Christians follow the teachings of Jesus Christ, who they believe was the Son of God.

DID YOU KNOW?

All followers of the Sikh religion wear or carry five symbols of their faith. These are: uncut hair, a comb, a steel bracelet, a sword, and short pants.

Islam

The followers of Islam are called Muslims. The Dome of the Rock in Jerusalem is one of their most holy sites. Muslims call God Allah, and they believe that the prophet Muhammed was Allah's messenger.

Hinduism

Hinduism began thousands of years ago in India. Its believers try to follow an ideal, or perfect, way of life. There are many Hindu gods, including Brahma, Vishnu, and Shiva.

A Hindu goddess

Cities of the sun

From 2,000 years ago, Central and South America were home to a number of powerful civilizations. The people built huge palaces for their rulers and massive temples for their gods. Many of these people worshipped the Sun as their god.

The Aztecs

In the 1400s, the Aztec people took over part of the country that today is called Mexico. They made beautiful cloth, baskets, and bowls, and wonderful gold jewelry. To please their gods they killed animals and people in special ceremonies called sacrifices.

DID YOU KNOW?

Long ago, the peoples of Central and South America did not use the wheel. Everything was carried by people or llamas.

Toltec warrior statues at the ruined city of Tula.

The Toltecs

About 1,000 years ago, the Toltec people ruled the land that is now central Mexico. The Toltecs had a powerful army, and they conquered all the people living around them. They also built large cities and carved huge statues of Toltec warriors.

The Incas' descendants still speak Quechua, the Inca language.

The Maya

The Maya lived in Central America about 3,500 years ago. Their civilization was at its greatest from 300 to 900 AD. The Maya built stepped pyramids. They wrote using signs and pictures instead of letters.

The Incas

The Incas lived in what is now Peru. One of their main cities was Cuzco. It had wide streets and large squares. The Inca empire included much of the western coast of South America. It collapsed after the Spanish invaded Peru in 1531.

Empires of the East

From about 1,000 years ago, huge empires grew in eastern lands. Their rulers had great wealth and power, and fought many battles. Skilled people made beautiful pots, paintings, and statues, and built many amazing buildings.

Riding to war

The warrior king Genghis Khan led his people, the Mongols, in many battles. The Mongols rode fast and fought fiercely. About 800 years ago they ruled most of Asia, but their power soon faded.

The great temple at Angkor.

DID YOU KNOW?

Genghis Khan ruled one of the biggest empires the world has ever seen, but he could not read or write.

The Great Wall

Over hundreds of years, the Chinese built the Great Wall of China to keep out raiders from the north. It ran across hills and valleys for around 3,700 miles. Today much of the Great Wall is in ruins, although some parts are in good condition.

Shoguns

Japan was ruled by an emperor but most of the power was held by the top general, or shogun. There were many wars as important families fought each other for power and to become shogun.

Largest temple

About 900 years ago the Khmer people of Southeast Asia built a giant temple at Angkor. With massive walls, over 1,000 yards long, and five huge towers, it is the largest religious building in the world.

Knights and castles

Between 1,100 and 600 years ago, many European kings built castles out of stone. Castles were designed to keep the people inside safe from attack. They often had thick stone walls, tall towers, and protective moats of water all around them.

Pretend battle

Knights were important soldiers who fought for their king. They sometimes practiced their skills in pretend fights called jousts. They used a long spear, called a lance, and a short sword.

Cannons

As cannons became more powerful, the days of the castle came to an end. Firing stone cannon balls, these weapons could knock big holes in the castle walls.

Well protected

A castle was more than a massive home. Often it was like a small village. Strong stone walls kept out enemies. Stores of food could last for months, and water came from a deep well.

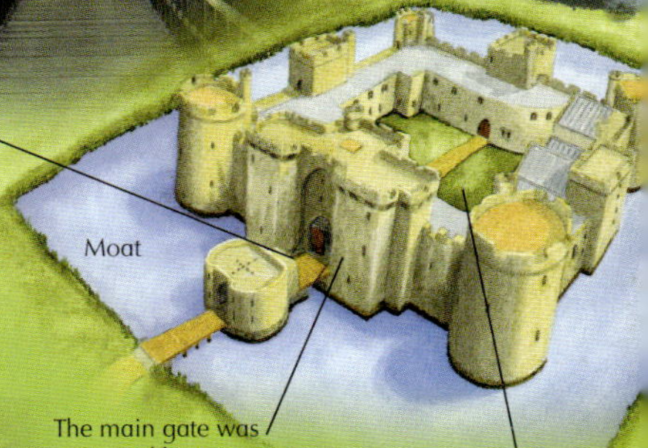

Life as a peasant

While the rich lived comfortable lives in their big houses or castles, ordinary people, called peasants, had hard lives. All their work was done by hand or using animals such as horses or cattle to pull plows or carry things.

Exploring new lands

Since earliest times, people have been curious to explore new lands, where the customs and ways of life are different. Some explorers sailed the seas in search of riches or adventure, while others searched for better places to live.

DID YOU KNOW?

The Vikings chose the name Greenland to make people want to go there. In fact, Greenland is a much icier and colder country than Iceland.

Across the Atlantic

In 1492, the Italian Christopher Columbus made his famous voyage of exploration to America. He visited many islands in the Caribbean. On his voyage he took three ships with him, the *Nina*, the *Pinta*, and the *Santa Maria*.

Viking explorers

The Vikings of Scandinavia sailed their longships to settle in new lands. They became the first Europeans to reach America. Evidence of a Viking village dating back 1,000 years has been found in L'Anse Aux Meadows in Newfoundland, Canada.

Travelers on the Silk Road today.

The Silk Road to China

Long ago, only the Chinese knew how to make silk. It was brought to Europe along a route called the Silk Road. In 1271, an Italian merchant called Marco Polo took this road to China where he met the great leader Kublai Khan.

The Maoris

There were no people in New Zealand until sailors from Polynesia arrived there just over 1,000 years ago. New Zealand's Maori people are the descendants of these explorers.

Maoris performing a "haka," a traditional war dance.

The New World

America was known as the New World because most people from Europe did not know about it until Christopher Columbus went there more than 500 years ago.

Native Americans

When the Europeans first arrived in the New World they found Native Americans already living there. Soon there were lots of battles as the Europeans wanted to take the land for themselves.

Early settlers

People from Europe set up homes along the east coast of North America. As their numbers increased, they began to move west. They traveled in covered wagons with all their possessions.

The wild west

The wide grassy plains of North America were so big, the farmers could let their cattle and horses graze freely. Each year the cowboys would round up the herds and take them to market.

DID YOU KNOW?

The USA's capital city, Washington D.C., is named after both George Washington and Christopher Columbus. D.C. stands for the District of Columbia.

Revolutionary War

North America was ruled by Britain, but the people wanted to run their own country. They began a fierce battle called the Revolutionary War, or the War of Independence. In 1783, the Americans won, and the United States of America (the USA) was born.

The Revolutionary War lasted over five years.

Smoke and steam

About 300 years ago, people in Europe started to invent many new machines, such as steam engines and weaving looms for making cloth. Factories were built, making all kinds of products. This period became known as the Industrial Revolution.

Steam power

The steam engine was first invented in about 1700. Then in 1769 the Scottish engineer James Watt made it better and stronger. Steam engines were soon being used to power factories. Later they were used to drive trains.

Steam locomotives are still in use all over the world.

Tallest tower

The Eiffel Tower is in Paris, France. It was built in 1889 to celebrate all the latest inventions of that time. It is over 1,000 feet tall and named after its builder, Gustave Eiffel.

Farm to factory

Before the Industrial Revolution, most people worked on farms and would spin and weave at home. When steam-powered machines made it possible to spin and weave cotton much faster, many people went to work in factories.

Building with iron and steel

During the Industrial Revolution, engineers used iron and steel to build longer bridges and safer tunnels than ever before. One of the most famous was the British engineer Isambard Kingdom Brunel, who built 25 railway lines and over 100 bridges.

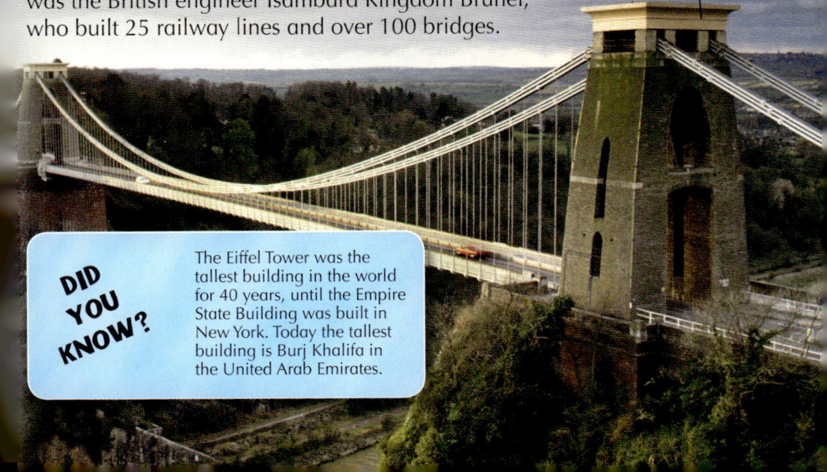

Brunel designed this bridge in 1830. It is called a suspension bridge.

DID YOU KNOW?

The Eiffel Tower was the tallest building in the world for 40 years, until the Empire State Building was built in New York. Today the tallest building is Burj Khalifa in the United Arab Emirates.

A changing world

The 20th century was a time of great change. There were two terrible wars, in which many millions of people were killed. New technology altered the way people lived their lives. People also began to travel more, and enjoy more leisure time.

British Spitfire fighter plane

Air power

The Wright Brothers invented the airplane in 1903. By the time World War II started in 1939, the airplane had already become a powerful weapon. After the war, lots of people began to travel by air purely for pleasure.

World War I

After many years of small battles in Europe, a bigger war started in 1914. This became known as World War I, or the Great War. It lasted for four years, and more than eight million soldiers died.

At the movies

The first films were made in black and white, and had no sound. But this did not stop comedians such as Charlie Chaplin becoming popular with people all over the world.

More than 15 million Model T Fords were made. Most of them were black.

The Ford Model T

By 1900, the first cars were on the roads. But they were slow and often broke down. The Ford Model T was the first car that ordinary people could afford to buy and that worked really well.

The Beatles

In the 1950s and '60s, a new type of music was created that appealed to young people. The Beatles from Liverpool, England, became an international sensation.

The world today

History is what happened in the past. The important people and events of today will one day become history. It is hard to tell exactly what things will be remembered. It could be a terrible war or discovering the cure to a deadly disease.

High-tech cities

Countries such as China, India, and Malaysia are developing fast. They are building new cities with all the latest technology.

Shanty towns

Around many new and wealthy cities poor people live in shanty towns. Here, the houses are shacks, made from garbage, and often with no running water or electricity.

Year 2000

A millennium is 1,000 years. In the year 2000 people all over the world held parties and set off fireworks to celebrate the New Millennium.

Trying to help

Lots of people in the richer countries want to help the people living in poorer countries. Big music festivals have been held to raise money for people who are hungry and to remind us about poor people.

Deadly drought

A long time without rain is called a drought. Farm crops die so the people have no food. In recent years, drought in Africa has killed millions of people.

The way we live

The world we live in is home to over seven billion people—and that number is growing by around 200,000 every day. All these people live in more than 200 different countries, spread over the continents of Africa, Asia, Australasia, Europe, North America, and South America. A few hardy scientists even live in Antarctica! If you wanted to say hello to everyone in the world, you would need to speak nearly 3,000 different languages.

The houses we live in

Around the world, people live in very different kinds of homes. Some people live in highrise city apartments, others in tents made of felt.

High homes

Cities are very crowded places, so many people live in apartments. Some of these are in very tall buildings. Hundreds of people may live in one apartment block.

Homes on sticks

In some parts of Southeast Asia, people build houses held up by strong wooden posts. This keeps the house clear of floods—and snakes. It also helps keep the house cool.

Keeping cool

In hot countries, houses have plenty of shady areas to help people stay cool. Houses are often painted white. The white walls throw back, or reflect, the heat of the Sun.

Mobile homes

Some people do not live in one place all the time. They are called nomads. Nomads usually live in tents that they can take down and carry. The nomads of Mongolia live in round tents called yurts. Yurts have a wooden frame, covered in felt, canvas, and cotton.

Mud houses

In Africa, houses are often made of mud. The mud is spread over a framework of sticks and then allowed to dry. But the mud can also be used to make bricks. It is pressed into brick-shaped boxes and dried in the sun.

What people wear

Clothes may keep us warm or cool. Some clothes are very comfortable, others are elegant or beautiful. Clothes can show that we belong to a particular group, such as a school or a team.

Shimmering sari

This beautiful silk dress comes from India. It is called a sari. It is a long piece of material that wraps around the body several times and drapes over the shoulder.

DID YOU KNOW?

Silk is made by silkworms. These are really caterpillars of the silk moth. They spin a casing, or cocoon, of silk to protect themselves before changing into moths.

Denim jeans

Jeans were created more than 100 years ago. They are made from a strong blue material called denim. Jeans were first designed as work pants for miners.

Bright colors

In many African countries the clothes are often brightly colored. They also have beautiful patterns and special stitching called embroidery. African clothes are usually loose and flowing, to keep people cool in the hot sunshine.

Stay cool

For thousands of years, in the hot Middle East, people have worn long, loose robes. The robes are often white, to "bounce back," or reflect, the heat of the Sun.

At school

In most countries, children are allowed to go to school all year round. But some children have to stop school at certain times of the year to help gather crops from the fields.

School clothes

In many schools, all the children wear the same kind of clothes as each other, called a uniform. This makes them feel part of the group.

Outdoor school

In countries where it is hot, or the people are poor, school is held out in the open. The children may even sit on the hard ground.

School bus

Children walk or bicycle to school, or go by car or bus. Often there is a special bus for school children. In snowy places children may ski or ride on a snow vehicle called a skidoo.

High-tech schools

In many schools, children have lots of things to help them learn, such as computers or books. But in some countries, children have to share books, or have no books at all.

Special schools

Some children go to schools where they have extra lessons to learn how to dance, sing, or practice sport. Other schools help children with special learning needs, such as deaf or blind people.

This is a special school for dance in Thailand.

At work

People go to work to earn money so they can pay for their food, clothes, and houses. Most people work only during the day, but others, such as doctors and police officers, also work at night.

In an office

Today, a lot of work is done in offices. People sit at a desk with a computer and a telephone. Computers are used for all kinds of office work, from writing letters and emails to doing really difficult math.

Skilled worker

Some people work with their hands to make or mend things. Carpenters work with wood, plumbers work with pipes, and electricians work with electricity.

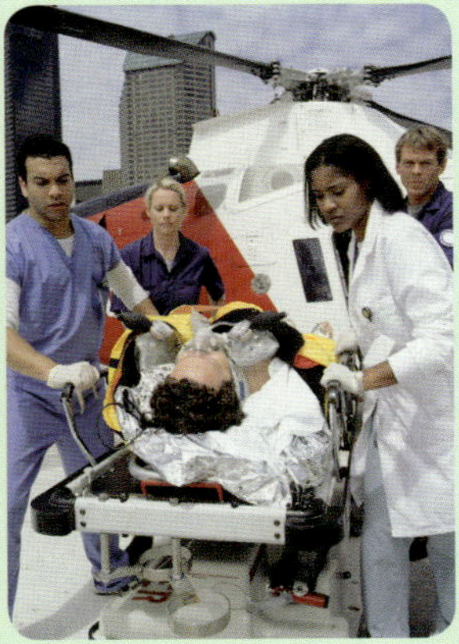

Emergency!

Police, firefighters, and ambulance crews are all part of the emergency services. Their work can often help to save lives. They must always be ready to help at any time of the day or night.

Animal doctor

Veterinarians are trained to work with animals. Some vets need to understand how lots of different animals' bodies work. Other vets work with one type of animal, such as horses.

In a factory

People who work in factories make things or put things together, such as bicycles. Some of the work may be done by hand, but a lot of it is done by machines.

On the move

In many countries most people own cars and use them every day. We call this private transportation. Buses, trains, boats, and planes are public transportation. In most poorer countries, people still walk or cycle everywhere.

Animal transport

When the ground is rough or steep, animals such as horses or donkeys often provide the best way to get around. In other parts of the world, llamas, yaks, camels, or water buffaloes are used to carry people and things.

Pedal power

An easy way to get around is by bicycle. In China there are more than one billion bicycles. Some pull small carts for carrying shopping.

DID YOU KNOW?

Bicycles are the world's most popular way of traveling. In the Netherlands there are almost as many bicycles as there are people.

On foot

For many people walking remains the only way they can travel. Some people have to walk many miles every day to go to school, work, or the market.

Going underground

In large towns and cities, the roads often become jammed with traffic. So some cities have trains that run under the ground. These can carry lots of people around a city very quickly.

Where food comes from

All the food you see on the supermarket shelves is first grown as crops, or raised as farm animals. Although machines do a lot of the work, millions of people still work hard to harvest the food we eat.

Planting rice is very hard work.

Growing rice

Rice feeds more people in the world than any other cereal crop. The rice plant likes to grow in very soggy fields, called paddies. Almost all rice is planted and harvested by hand.

Livestock farming

When farmers keep animals to work the land or to sell for meat, we call it "livestock" farming. Some of the biggest farms in the world raise cows that give us the meat we call beef. Sheep give us lamb, and pigs give us pork and ham.

Picking by hand

Tomatoes and other soft fruit are picked by hand because they are soft and easily squashed. Strawberries and plums are also picked this way. This is because the fruit does not all ripen at the same time, so people have to choose which fruit to pick.

Seafood

Fishing boats called trawlers drag huge nets through the ocean to catch fish and other sea creatures. When they are full, the nets are pulled onto the boat and the catch is emptied onto the boat deck.

DID YOU KNOW?

Some food is produced in a natural way. This is called organic food. The crops are not sprayed with chemicals, and the animals eat foods without chemical additives.

The food we eat

Long ago, people ate only what they could grow, catch, or hunt themselves. Today, supermarkets sell food from all around the world. This means we can eat food such as strawberries all year round and not just when they are in season.

Preparing food

Food such as fish must be cleaned carefully to be ready for cooking. This fish has had its head, tail, scales, and bones cut away. The fleshy parts that are left are called fillets.

Steaming

In New Zealand, there are lots of hot springs and steaming geysers. These underground water sources are naturally hot. The Maoris use the water to cook their food and keep it warm.

Eat in, take out

Today, people cook at home less often. We go out to eat in restaurants or buy takeout food, such as pizza or burgers and fries, to eat almost anywhere.

Cooked over a fire

In some areas, people do not have electricity or gas. They cook meals in a big pot over an open fire. It can take hours to collect the firewood.

Based on rice

In eastern countries, many meals include rice. Rice can be steamed and served with a hot, spicy curry, or made with milk and sugar into a dessert. In fact, some people eat rice for breakfast, lunch, and dinner.

DID YOU KNOW?

One of the most costly foods is caviar. It is the tiny black eggs from a large fish called a sturgeon. The best caviar costs more than a new bicycle. It tastes very salty.

Stores and markets

There are as many different kinds of stores as there are things to buy. Some, called department stores, sell all kinds of things, from clothes to beds. Others specialize in selling just one thing.

Shopping malls

A mall is a group of shops all together under one roof. You stay warm and dry, and you can "window shop." This means looking at things on display without buying them.

On display

In hot, dry countries many shopkeepers put all their goods outside. As people pass by, they can see everything that is for sale.

This shop in Morocco sells metal pots, trays, and candlesticks.

Where supermarkets get their food from

Before food reaches the shelves of your local supermarket, it has to go on a long journey. First it is grown or raised on a farm (1). Then it is taken to a huge building, called a warehouse (2). From here it goes to the supermarket. Only then can you put it into your supermarket cart (3).

Markets

A market is usually an open area with many small stalls that sell lots of different things. In some markets the food is displayed on the ground.

Playing sports

Playing sports keeps you active and healthy. You can play as part of a team or by yourself. Sports help people to learn about themselves. They learn how to lose without being upset, and how to win without being big-headed. Most of all, sports are a lot of fun.

Skiing

Skis allow you to slide over the snow really fast. Sometimes you can even jump through the air.

Sport for all

Everyone is suited to some type of athletics, even people with disabilities. People in wheelchairs can play and enjoy a wide variety of sports, including archery, basketball, and racing. Some wheelchair athletes compete in marathon races.

Soccer

The sport that is played most around the world is soccer. It is a team sport, with 11 players in each team. Every four years the best countries play against each other to try and win the World Cup.

DID YOU KNOW?

The biggest sporting event in the world is the Olympic Games. These Games happen every four years. Almost 4,000 people take part in more than 25 different sports.

Run and jump

Athletes who run short races very quickly are called sprinters. Sometimes sprinters have to jump over hurdles as well.

Music, dance, and art

Most people like to be creative in some way. They may like to sing, dance, play an instrument, or paint. These activities are called the arts. You don't have to be really good at the arts—the important thing is to enjoy them.

Breakdancers jump around and even spin on their heads.

Breakdancing

There are as many kinds of dance as there are music. Some dances are slow and serious. Some, like breakdancing, is very energetic.

Traditional dance

Some types of music and dance are thousands of years old. These Tibetan dancers are performing at one of their summer festivals.

Art everywhere

Ever since the first person drew the outline of an animal on a cave wall, people have loved to paint. A few paintings are so valuable they are kept locked up. Others help brighten up drab city streets.

Plan of a modern orchestra

A large group of musicians who play classical music is called an orchestra. Most orchestras have violins (1) and (2), horns (3), clarinets (4), oboes (5), flutes (6), bassoons (7), violas (8), cellos (9), percussion (10), trumpets (11), trombones (12), tubas (13), double-basses (14).

This statue is called the Strongman. It is in Japan.

Sculptures

Many artists like to carve figures out of wood or stone. These sculptures can look very real. Around the world, sculptures can be seen in cities and parks, as well as in art galleries.

Ceremonies and festivals

In every country of the world people celebrate special days in different ways. It could be a noisy celebration at the beginning of a new year, or it could be a religious day when everyone goes to a special place to pray.

Chinese New Year

The Chinese New Year is usually around the end of January or the beginning of February. The celebrations traditionally last for 15 days. People dress up and there are lots of fireworks.

Festival of light

Diwali is the Hindu festival of light. It is celebrated every year between the end of October and the middle of November. Hindus all over the world celebrate by lighting candles.

This nativity scene was actually performed in Bethlehem, the place of Christ's birth.

The birth of Christ

At Christmas, the birth of Christ in a stable in Bethlehem is celebrated by Christians all over the world. The story of Christ's birth, or nativity, is often acted out in schools and churches.

DID YOU KNOW?

The Hindu Great Fair on the banks of the River Ganges is the greatest gathering of people in the world. Up to 20 million people go there every year.

Prayer time

Followers of some religions go to a place of worship once a week, but Muslims have to pray five times a day. They kneel and face toward the holy city of Mecca.

Running our lives

Most countries are looked after by a group of people called a government. It is the government that makes laws and takes big decisions such as how much to spend on hospitals, roads, and schools.

Governments meet to discuss things in a special debating room.

Lots of meetings

The government of a country meets often to talk, or debate, and make decisions. Usually there is one main leader who has the final decision. This can be a president or a prime minister.

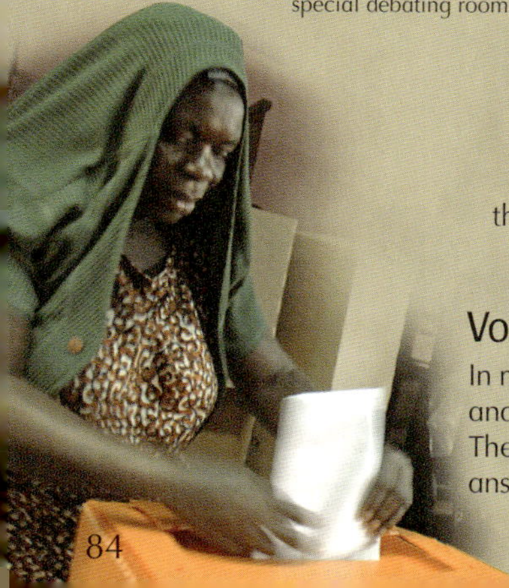

Voting

In many countries people choose their leaders and the people they want in the government. They choose in secret and then post their answers in a special box. This is called voting.

Kings and queens

In some countries the leaders are kings, queens, or emperors. They have power because they are part of an important family. Sometimes the government helps them to look after, or run, the country.

United Nations

Almost every country in the world is a member of a big organization called the United Nations. They meet to sort out arguments between countries and help when there are famines or earthquakes.

Taking over

If there are great problems in a country, the army may take over. They make new laws and keep control. This is called a coup.

Animals and plants

Life is all around us. Wherever we look, we see animals, plants, and other living things. Animals are living because they grow, have babies, and move about. Some of them burrow in soil or swim in water. Others run on the ground, slither among rocks, or fly in the air. Plants are also alive. They may not move around in the way animals do, but they grow and produce baby plants.

Simple plants

There are millions of kinds of plants. They grow everywhere, from the tops of mountains to the seabed. Some are smaller than this letter "o," others grow as tall as small skyscrapers.

Ferns and mosses

Ferns have wavy-edged fronds. Mosses have tiny green leaves. Both ferns and mosses like damp, shady places. Too much sunshine dries them out.

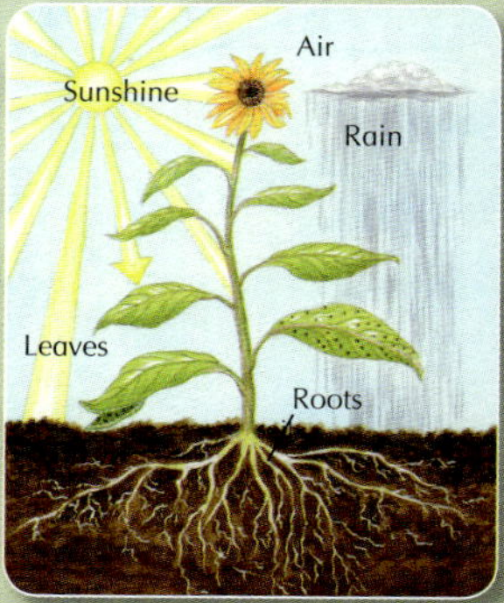

Plants and growth

Plants must have sunlight and air to grow. They take these in through their leaves. Plants also need water and special food called minerals. Most plants take these from the soil, through their roots.

Seaweeds

Seaweeds do not have flowers and many kinds do not even have roots, but float in the sea. Some seaweeds are harvested for food. Others, such as wrack, are used to make toothpaste and ice cream.

Wrack seaweed

This stag-horn fern grows on trees.

Air plants

Some plants do not need the soil to grow. Instead, they use their roots to cling to trees or other plants. These types of plants are sometimes called air plants. They get their water from dew and rain.

Fascinating fungi

Both mushrooms and toadstools are types of fungi. Fungi are not plants, but they are not animals either. They grow in damp places and feed on the rotting remains of dead plants and animals.

Flowers

Some flowers are bright and beautiful, while others are tiny and hidden. Flowers help make seeds so that new flowers can grow. But the seeds can't grow on their own. They need dust-like grains called pollen from another flower of the same kind.

Buds and flowers

Flowers come out of small green buds. The colored parts of a flower are called petals. In different flowers the petals can be white, yellow, orange, red, blue, or even black.

How poppies make their seeds

Seeds are made in the middle of the flowers. Pollen grains travel from one poppy and land on another. The part of the flower that contains the seeds then starts to grow and, one by one, the petals fall off. Holes open up in the seed pod and allow the seeds to fall out when the wind blows.

How pollen moves

Some flowers let the wind carry their pollen to other flowers. But many flowers need animals to do this. The flowers make sweet nectar, which bees and other creatures love. As these animals drink the nectar, they get covered in pollen, which they carry to the next flower.

Dandelion seeds have fluffy parachutes that are carried by the wind.

Spreading seeds

Some seeds are small and light, and blow away in the wind. Other seeds have tasty parts that animals eat. The animal drops the rest of the seed on the soil, where it grows into a new plant.

Trees

Trees are the biggest plants of all. They are tall and strong, with lots of branches. They give us wood, fruit, and nuts, as well as shade on a hot day.

Fruit

Much of the fruit that we eat grows on trees. Certain types of fruit, such as oranges, can be grown all year round in some parts of the USA.

Leaves in summer

In summer, trees such as the oak, beech, and this fruit tree, have green leaves. But in the fall, when the weather becomes cold, the leaves turn brown and fall off. New leaves grow again in spring, when the warm weather returns.

Leaves all year

Evergreen trees, such as the pine, have leaves on them all year round. Their leaves do drop off, but new leaves grow all the time. Pine leaves are long and thin, like needles. Pine tree seeds grow inside cones.

Pinecones carry seeds.

DID YOU KNOW?

When a tree is cut down you can see inside the tree trunk. Circles of wood start from the center and grow out. If you count these rings, you can tell how old the tree is.

Nuts

Many trees, including the hazel, walnut, and beech, produce seeds called nuts that we like to eat. Oak trees produce nuts called acorns. People can't eat acorns, but they are popular with squirrels and other woodland animals.

Simple animals

Many animals have very simple bodies, without a bony skeleton. Some have no legs, while others have lots of bendy "arms" called tentacles. Most simple animals are harmless, but a few can give you a painful sting.

Living in soil

Earthworms live in the ground. They burrow their way through the soil and feed on any tiny pieces of dead, rotting plants that they come across. Earthworms are good for the garden, because the tunnels they make let air and rain into the soil.

Sliming along

Snails leave a trail of sticky slime as they slide along. They come out at night when it is cool and damp, to eat leaves and other parts of plants.

DID YOU KNOW?

Simple animals do not have bones in their back. This means they can't grow very big, unless they live in the sea. The giant octopus can grow up to 19 feet long and weigh more than 110 pounds.

Simple but smart

The octopus is probably the most intelligent of the simple animals. It can even open boxes and jars with its eight suckered tentacles.

Jellyfish

The jellyfish floats in the ocean. It can swim slowly by squeezing its umbrella-shaped body. The jellyfish trails its long stinging tentacles behind it to catch small fish and shrimps.

Sea anemone

The sea anemone looks like a flower, but it is really an animal. This ocean creature clings to a rock and uses its tentacles to sting small fish and push them into its mouth.

Lots of legs

Some animals have six legs, or eight, or even more. Counting an animal's legs can tell us what kind of creature it is. If a minibeast has six legs, it is likely to be an insect. If it has eight legs, then it is probably a spider.

Tarantula

Swallowtail butterfly

Eight legs

Spiders, such as this tarantula, have eight legs. Spiders hunt other creatures and kill them by injecting poison with their needle-sharp fangs. Some spiders chase after or jump on their prey, but others spin sticky webs to catch insects to eat.

DID YOU KNOW?

Crabs wave at each other! A crab has eight legs and two big claws. It waves its claws at other crabs to warn them to stay away or face a fight.

Most legs

The animal that has the most legs is the millipede. Some millipedes have as many as 750 legs! Although they have lots of legs, millipedes move quite slowly. They like to munch on dead leaves and rotting wood.

Many legs

The giant centipede lives in North America. It is speedy and bendy, and grows 12 inches long. It catches and eats cockroaches, crickets, mice, and baby birds.

Giant centipede

Six legs

All insects have six legs, and most have wings, too. There are more insects in the world than any other type of animal, from scurrying ants to buzzing bees and beautiful butterflies sipping sweet nectar.

Fish and amphibians

Fish have fins and a tail, and swim in water. The biggest fish is the whale shark of the open ocean. It is 40 feet long, which is as big as a bus. One of the smallest fish is the goby that lives in jungle swamps. This tiny fish can be as small as your fingernail.

Great white shark

Ocean hunter

The great white shark is the biggest hunting fish. It has 50 razor-sharp teeth and eats fish, sea birds, seals, and dolphins. Only rarely does it attack people.

Fast swimmers

Fish have smooth, "streamlined" bodies tha help them swim easil through the water. Th sailfish can swim faste than 60 miles an hou

Amphibians

Amphibians are animals that live in water when they are young. When they are fully grown, they spend most of their time on land. Frogs, toads, newts, and salamanders are all amphibians.

From frog spawn to adult frog

Female frogs can lay a lot of eggs, sometimes up to 4,000. The baby frogs that hatch out are called tadpoles.

Young tadpoles have a tail but no legs. As they grow, the tail shrinks and their front and back legs appear.

Scaly reptiles

There are many kinds of reptiles. Lizards have four legs and can run fast. Snakes have no legs and slither quietly. Crocodiles and alligators are big, strong, and toothy. Turtles have a hard body shell. Most reptiles have scaly skin, and their babies hatch from eggs.

Big bite

A crocodile hides in muddy water, waiting for an animal to come for a drink. When the animal bends down to take a sip, the crocodile grabs it with its huge jaws. Then it drags the animal under the water to drown it.

Color change

The chameleon is a lizard that can change the color of its skin to blend in with its background. This helps it hide from danger and ambush insects, which it catches with its long, sticky tongue.

Ready to strike

Snakes bite other animals using long, sharp teeth, called fangs. They can't chew, so they swallow their meal whole. The cobra is a poisonous snake. It can flatten the skin on its neck, called its hood, and rear up to make itself look more frightening.

Danger on the beach

Female sea turtles lay their eggs on beaches and bury them in the sand. The baby turtles hatch and dig their way to the surface. They must hurry to the sea, or they may be eaten by crabs, seagulls, and lizards.

Birds

The bald eagle has a wingspan of around $6\frac{1}{2}$ feet.

Birds live all over the world, from jungles and deserts to the open ocean. They all have feathers, a beak, two legs for walking, and two wings for flapping. But not all birds can fly. Penguins use their wings to swim and ostriches use their strong legs to run fast.

Big bird

The ostrich is the biggest bird of all. It's taller and heavier than an adult person. An ostrich can't fly, but it can run faster than a racehorse. Its eggs are 24 times larger than a hen's egg.

Eggs and chicks

Most birds build nests for their eggs. After they hatch, the baby birds, called chicks, open their beaks wide ready for food. The parent birds bring them food such as berries, flies, caterpillars, and worms.

DID YOU KNOW?

Owls have such big eyes that they cannot roll them from side to side. But the owl can turn its head in almost a full circle to see what is happening behind.

Flying high in the sky

A bird flaps its wings to push itself through the air. If there are warm currents of air, birds like the eagle can glide or soar without flapping. The eagle is a hunter. It has huge eyes to see animals far below.

Good swimmers

Penguins live in cold southern oceans. They flap their wings to swim fast through the water as they chase food such as fish, squid, and shrimps. Penguins lay their eggs and raise their chicks on land. Their thick feathers keep them warm even in the coldest weather.

Mammals on land

Mammals are animals with fur that feed their babies on milk. Many pets and farm animals are mammals, including dogs, cats, rabbits, cows, and sheep. People are mammals, too. Mammals are warm-blooded. This means that they can move around and stay active even in cold weather.

Flying in the dark

Bats are the only mammals that can fly. They also have such good hearing that they can fly in the dark. Some bats catch moths, mice, or fish. Others feed on soft fruit.

Mother's milk

A baby mammal feeds only on its mother's milk. Feeding on milk helps the young mammal to grow very quickly. It also means that the youngster must stay close to its mother, which helps keep it safe.

Fastest runner

The cheetah is the fastest mammal. It uses its speed to hunt other animals, such as gazelles. It can run faster than 60 miles an hour. But it can only do this for a short while, then it must rest.

DID YOU KNOW?

The elephant is the biggest land mammal. It weighs more than 5 tons—that's as much as 80 people!

Looking out for each other

Many grazing animals, such as antelopes, buffaloes, and wild horses, live together in large herds. This helps keep them safe, because there are many more eyes to watch out for prowling wolves, lions, or leopards.

Mammals in the ocean

Most mammals have four legs and a tail. But mammals that live in the ocean, such as whales and dolphins, have fins and flippers instead of legs. Ocean mammals must come to the surface to breathe air. Unlike fish, they can't breathe under water.

Leaping out

Dolphins love to leap out of the water and splash back in. They chase after food such as fish and squid. Dolphins talk to each other by making clicks, squeaks, and squeals.

Cow of the sea

The manatee is also called the sea cow. It munches underwater plants such as seagrass, just like a cow eating grass on land.

Fighting on the shore

Seals come ashore to have their babies. The biggest seal is the elephant seal. The males fight to rule over part of the beach. The mothers and babies must stay away from the fighting, so they don't get squashed.

Whales

The biggest whales, such as the humpback, have a mouth full of comblike plates called baleen. They use the baleen to sieve out their food from the ocean. Even though the whales are huge, they mostly eat tiny shrimps called krill.

DID YOU KNOW?

Ocean mammals and fish swim in quite different ways. Fish swish their tails from side to side. Ocean mammals beat their tails up and down.

Food and feeding

What an animal eats affects how and where it lives. Animals that eat plants are known as herbivores. Animals that eat other creatures are called carnivores. Some animals eat both plants and other creatures. These are known as omnivores.

Carnivores

Carnivores such as lions, tigers, and leopards are expert hunters. They have good senses to help them find their prey, and sharp teeth or claws for killing it.

Herbivores

Some herbivores, including impalas, graze on grass. Others, such as giraffes, nibble leaves off trees and shrubs. Many herbivores only feed at night, to keep them safe from carnivores.

Omnivores

Badgers will eat anything from an earthworm to roots, shoots, and berries. This diet helps badgers live in places where other animals would not find enough food.

A food chain

Big animals feed on smaller animals, which themselves eat even smaller animals. This is called a food chain.

Living together

Oxpeckers are birds that like to ride on the backs of big herbivores such as water buffaloes. As the buffaloes graze, they disturb insects, and the birds fly down to eat them.

Threats to nature

The biggest danger to nature is people. Around the world, people are hunting animals for their meat and skin, and damaging the natural places where plants and wild animals live.

Too much garbage

Every day we throw away huge amounts of garbage, from old televisions to candy wrappers. Much of it is harmful to nature. All this trash has to be taken away and either burned or buried in the ground.

Fewer wild places

Every year there are more people in the world. They all need somewhere to live and food to eat. This means that more wild places are being destroyed so that houses can be built and food crops grown. It also means that there are fewer places for wild animals to live and wild plants to grow.

Warmer world

We burn fuels in our homes, cars, factories, and power stations. This releases gases into the air that make the world warmer. Global warming could melt the ice where polar bears live.

DID YOU KNOW? There are less than 400 Sumatran rhinoceroses left. If people do not work hard to save them, they will soon all die out.

Saving nature

Wildlife parks and reserves are special places set aside for animals and plants. Wardens protect the animals from hunters.

This rhino has been put to sleep so it can be moved to a wildlife park, where it will be safe.

You and your body

Your body is amazing. You can run and jump using your muscles. You can see, hear, smell, touch, and taste with your five senses. And you can solve puzzles with your brain. Your body also does things without you even knowing! All the time—even when you are asleep—your heart is beating, your blood flowing. And if you hurt yourself, your body quickly tries to make itself better.

On the outside

Your skin covers your body all over. It helps protect you from small knocks and scrapes, germs and the harmful rays of the Sun. And when your skin does get cut or scratched, it even repairs itself.

Waterproof

Your skin stops water from getting into your body when you go swimming. But it does let water out through tiny holes called pores. We call this sweating and it helps cool you down.

Fingerprints

The skin on your hands is covered with lines and creases that help you hold things tightly. These lines make up little patterns. The ones on your fingertips are called fingerprints. What is amazing about these is that every person's fingerprints are different.

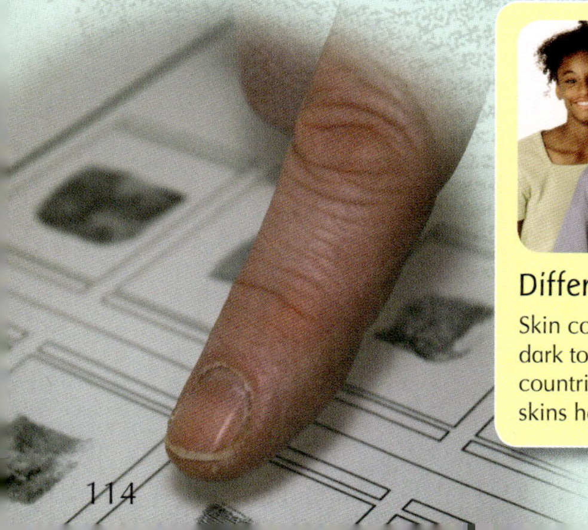

Different colors

Skin comes in lots of different colors, from dark to light. People who live in hot, sunny countries often have darker skins. Darker skins help prevent skin from burning.

Your skin

The tough outside layer of your skin is actually dead. Bits rub off all the time, but new skin is always growing, too. Hairs grow through the skin. They are attached to nerves to help you feel things.

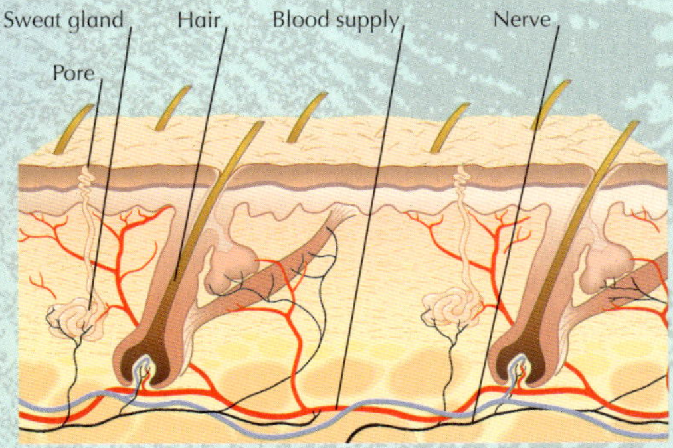

Your hair

You have hair all over your body. The tiny hairs on your arms help you feel things. The hair on your head keeps you warm. The color of your hair, and whether it is straight, curly, or wavy, will depend on what your parents' or grandparents' hair is like.

Bony parts

Your bones are strong and hard. They hold up the softer parts of your body. Your muscles move your bones. All of your bones together are called your skeleton.

Bone shapes

Different bones have different shapes. The longest bone is your upper leg, or thigh bone. The widest bone is your hip. The main bone inside your head is your skull.

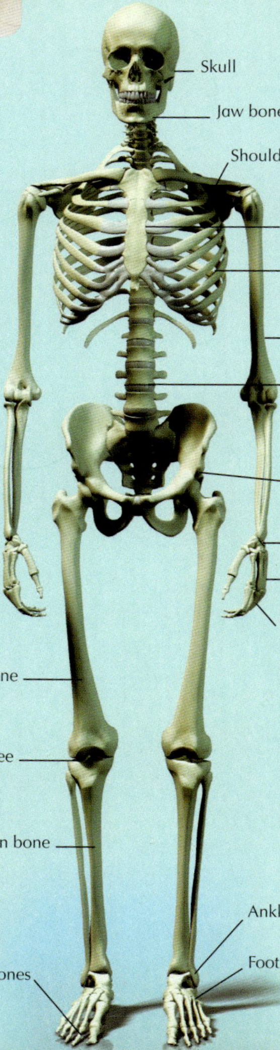

DID YOU KNOW?

A young baby has about 350 bones. As it grows, some of the bones join together. This is why an adult has only 206 bones.

Hip joint

At the point where your thigh meets your hip there is a joint called a ball joint. This allows the thigh bone to move in almost every direction.

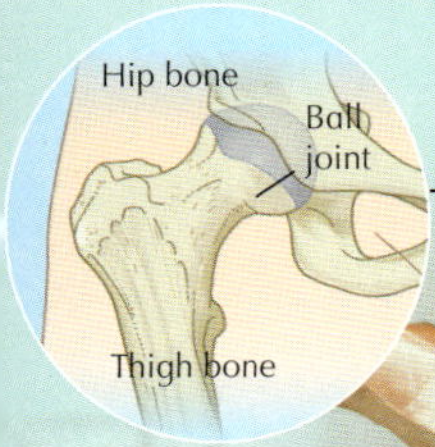

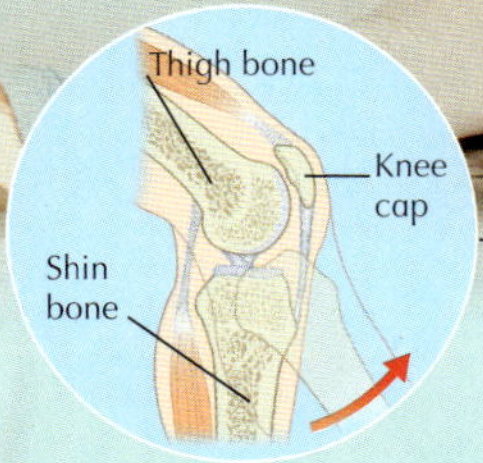

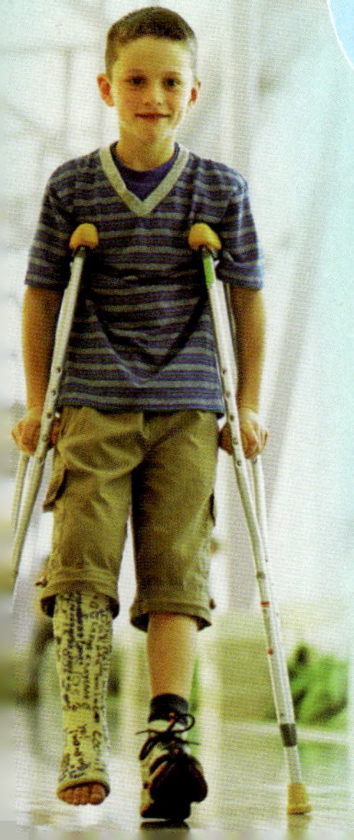

Joints

A joint is where two bones come together. Some joints, like your ankle, can only move a little. Others, such as your shoulder joint, can move in almost every direction.

Knee joint

The knee joint is a simple hinge joint. It works like the hinge on a door. This means that it can only bend one way.

Broken bones

Old dead bones look white and dry. But inside the body, bones are alive and busy. They can even mend themselves if they break, often with help from a strong support, or "cast," made of plaster.

Lots of muscles

Every time you move, you use your muscles. Even when you are sitting still, your muscles are busy working. You are still breathing and blinking, and your heart carries on beating. All of these actions use muscles.

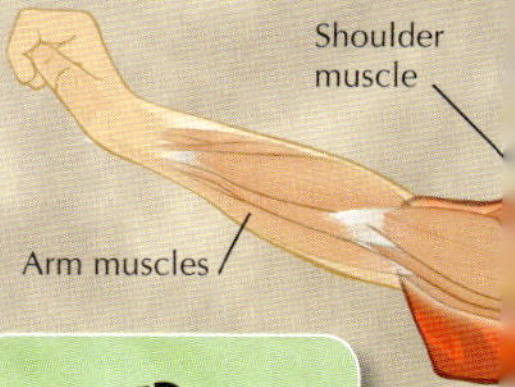

Powerful muscles

Muscles come in all shapes and sizes. Some muscles are large and powerful. Lifting weights can make your muscles stronger.

DID YOU KNOW?

You have hundreds of muscles in your body—in fact, about 640. Your muscles make up almost half your body weight.

The biggest muscle is in the buttock (bottom).

Muscle power

Most muscles are joined to a bone at each end. When the muscle gets shorter, it pulls on the bones and makes your joints move. Usually several muscles pull together for each movement.

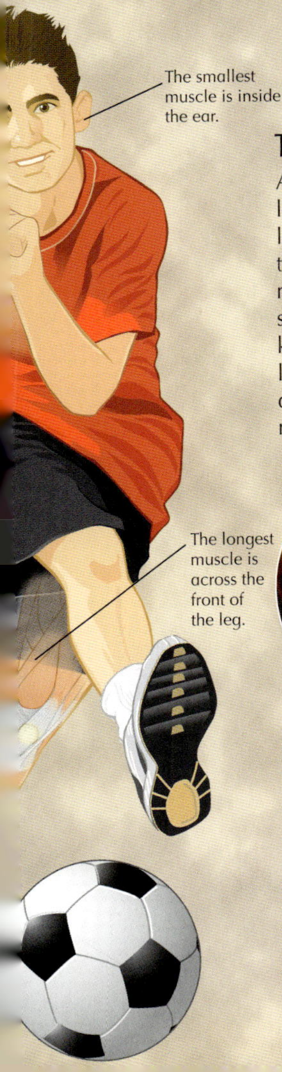

Tireless legs

Athletes who run long distances have longer, thinner muscles than weightlifters. These muscles may not be so big, but they can keep working for much longer. This helps the athletes to run long races without tiring.

Face it

You have more than 60 muscles in your head and around your eyes, nose, and mouth. You use these to make your face move. Try looking surprised, happy, or sad. Can you feel the muscles working?

Breathing

What do you do all the time, yet hardly ever think about? You breathe—in and out, all day and all night. This is because your body needs a gas called oxygen, which is in the air all around you.

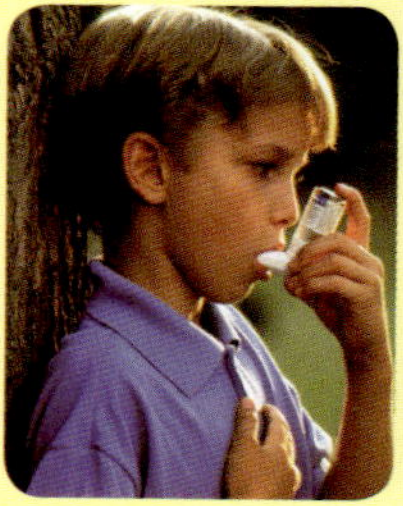

Inhaler

People with an illness called asthma often need to use an inhaler to help them breathe more easily.

Breathing in, breathing out

As you breathe in, air flows into two spongy bags in your chest called lungs. Your lungs take in the oxygen from the air and release the waste carbon dioxide gas, which you breathe out.

Your lungs are like two balloons that fill with air when you breathe in.

Air

You need to breathe air all the time. So if you swim under water you either have to hold your breath or breathe through a tube called a snorkel.

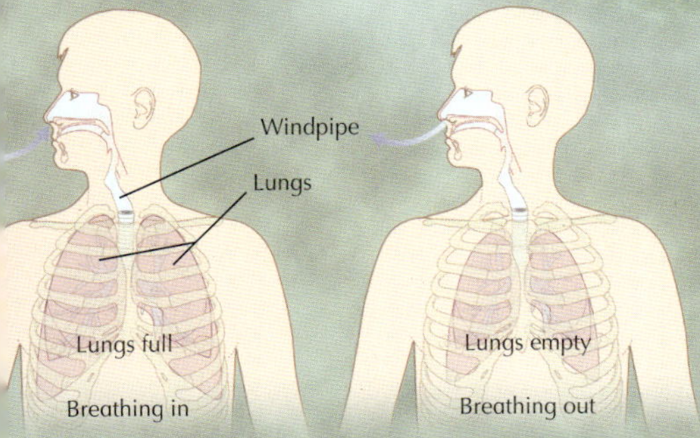

Voice box

When you talk, sing, or shout, you use your voice box. Air coming up the windpipe from your lungs shakes the voice box to make the sounds. Opera singers train their voices so they can sing loudly.

The lungs

You normally breathe in and out through your nose. As you breathe in, the ribs in your chest move upward and outward. Air passes down your windpipe and fills up your lungs. When you breathe out, your chest moves downward and inward, pushing the air out of your lungs.

Blood

Blood flows all around your body. Pumped by the heart, it never stops moving. Its main job is to carry oxygen, and the special substances called nutrients from food, all around your body.

Blood vessels

Blood vessels are the tubes that carry blood all around the body. Arteries are blood vessels carrying blood with fresh oxygen. Veins carry blood containing waste carbon dioxide.

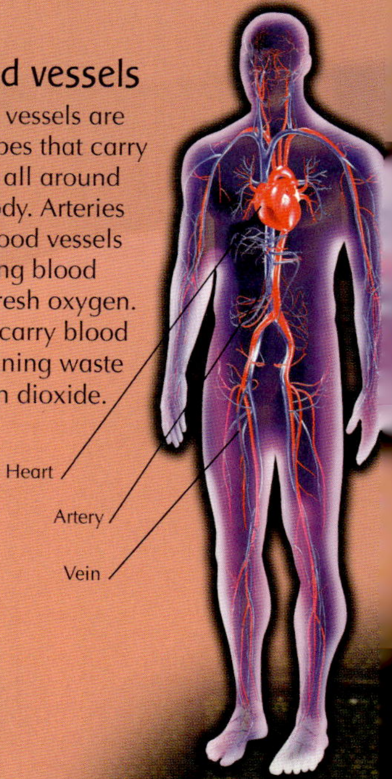

Testing blood

Sometimes when you are sick a nurse may take a few drops of your blood for a test. Blood often carries germs or other signs of illness that can help a doctor understand why you are unwell.

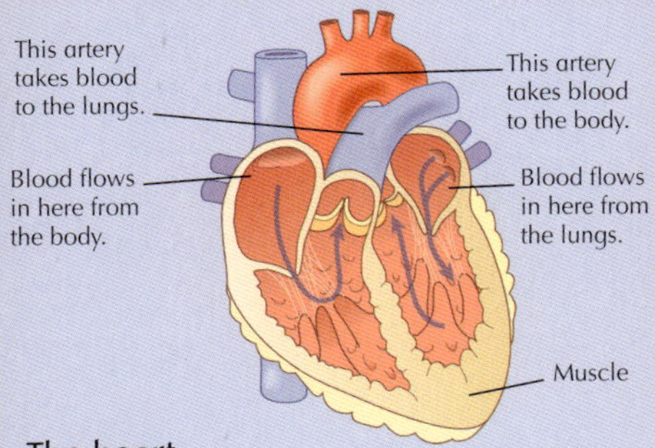

The heart

The heart is a large muscle. It works like a pump, sucking blood in and then pushing it out. The left side of the heart pumps the blood around the body. The right side of the heart pumps the blood around the lungs.

Stopping the flow

When you cut yourself you bleed. The blood helps to clean the wound as it flows out of the cut. Then special parts of the blood called platelets stick together to quickly stop the bleeding and form a scab.

Healthy heart

The heart is a muscle, so one way to keep it healthy and strong is to do any kind of exercise that makes it beat faster. When you are resting your heart beats about 60 to 90 times a minute. But when you play a sport it can beat twice as fast.

Eating and drinking

Your body needs food and water to work properly. Food contains special substances called nutrients. These give you energy and help your body grow and repair itself.

Why do you eat?

Food gives you more than just the energy to keep you going. It also contains vitamins and minerals. These are special nutrients that keep you healthy. That is why you need to eat lots of different types of food.

Lots of water

Nearly two-thirds of your body is made up of water. So you need to drink plenty of water every day. Some food also contains lots of water, especially fruit and vegetables, such as melons and carrots. If you get very hot, your body sweats to cool down. Sweat is mostly water. So if you sweat, you need to drink more.

Where does food go?

After you have swallowed your food, it goes down a long tube, called the gullet, to your stomach. Here special juices take all the goodness out of it. The parts your body can't use are then passed through more tubes, called the intestine, to your rectum.

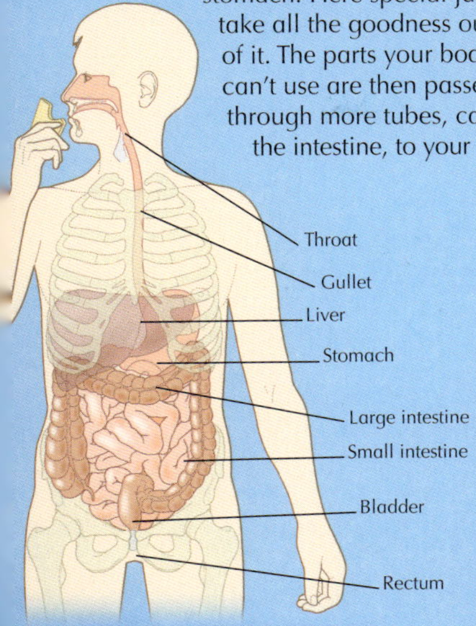

How many teeth?

Young children usually grow 20 teeth. From the age of about six years these first teeth fall out, and a new set of 32 adult teeth grows. Teeth need brushing every day to keep them healthy and clean.

DID YOU KNOW?

If you could take all the water out of an adult human body, it would fill half a bathtub!

On the potty

When you need to get rid of waste food and water you go to the toilet. Babies can't control when they go, so they wear diapers. Young children who are too small to use the toilet use a potty.

Seeing and hearing

You have five senses. These are sight, hearing, smell, touch, and taste. Sight and hearing are perhaps the most important. They allow you to see the world around you, and hear what's going on.

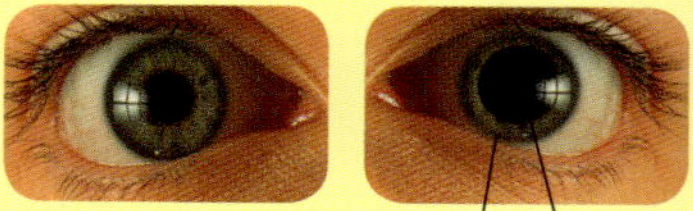

Wide open

Light enters the eye through a hole called the pupil. The colored part around it is called the iris. In normal light the pupil is quite small (left). In poor light the pupil gets bigger (right) so that more light is let in.

Too much noise

Your ears hear all kinds of sounds, from a quiet whisper to a huge crack of thunder. But some sounds, such as very loud music, can damage our hearing.

DID YOU KNOW?

Your ears actually help you to ride a bike! This is because parts of the ear called the semicircular canals have nothing to do with hearing. Instead they help you to balance.

High pitched

Your ears can hear a wide range of sounds, from the very low to the very high. But, as people get older, they find it harder to hear the highest sounds. Most adults can't hear the high-pitched squeaks of bats—but most children can!

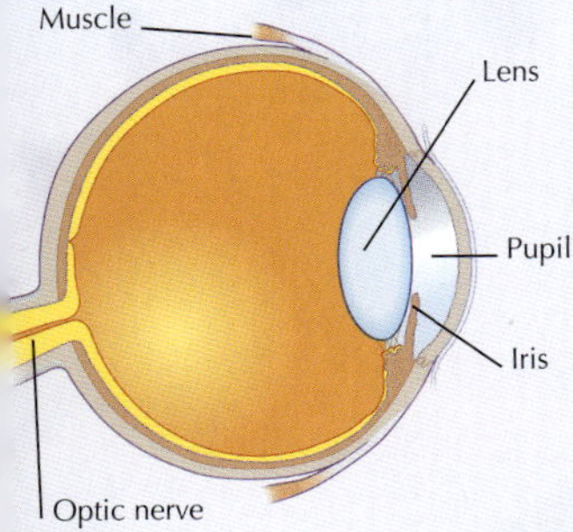

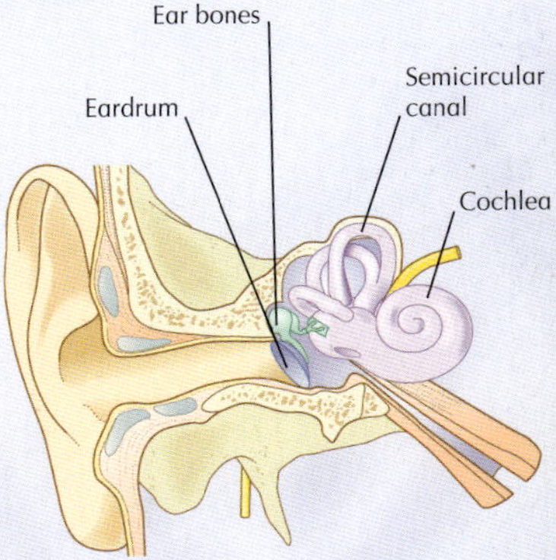

Inside the eye

As light enters the pupil, a lens, just like the lens on a pair of glasses, focuses the light. This makes what you see nice and clear. The eye then sends this picture along the optic nerve to your brain.

Inside the ear

Sounds hit a piece of skin in the ear called the eardrum. They then travel through three tiny ear bones to a snail-shaped part of the ear called the cochlea. From here the sounds travel along nerves to your brain.

Smell and taste

Smell and taste tell you about the foods you eat. They can also warn you of danger. You can smell smoke from a house on fire, long before you feel the heat of the flames. You can taste when food is rotten before eating enough to give yourself a tummy ache.

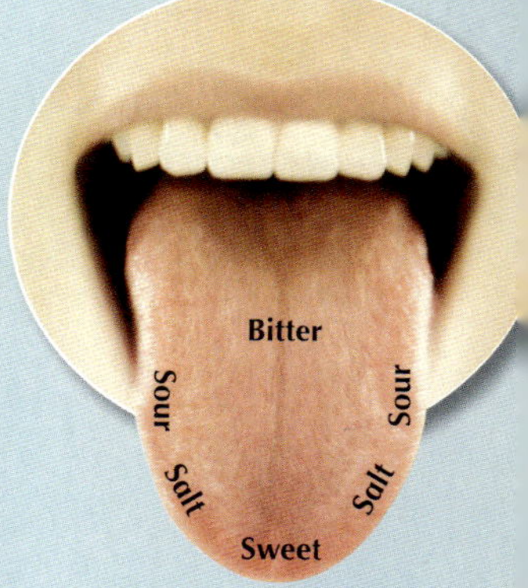

Your tongue's taste buds

Your tongue is covered in thousands of taste buds. These are like tiny taste detectors. Taste buds on different parts of the tongue recognize different kinds of taste.

Wide open

Smell and taste often work together. When you bite into an apple, you recognize its taste at once. But if you shut your eyes and pinch your nose, so that you can't smell, you will not be able to tell an apple from a raw potato!

If you have a bad cold, all your food can taste the same.

Happy smells

Tiny parts of the things you smell float in the air around you. When these tiny parts enter your nose, your brain recognizes them as smells. Lovely smells, like flowers, make you feel happy.

Sweet and sour

Young people usually prefer sweet tastes such as chocolate. As we get older, our tastes change so that we prefer sour, bitter, and even very spicy tastes.

Chocolate tastes sweet.

Lemons taste sour.

Nose for work

Some people use their noses in their jobs. The people who have to pick the best-tasting tea, coffee, and wine use their sense of smell more than their sense of taste. People who make perfumes also need a good sense of smell. We call these people "noses."

Your brain

If you could see inside your head, then you might think that your brain isn't very exciting. It looks like pink-gray gelatin. But your brain is really quite amazing, because it controls your whole body. It's also where you think, have ideas, learn, and remember.

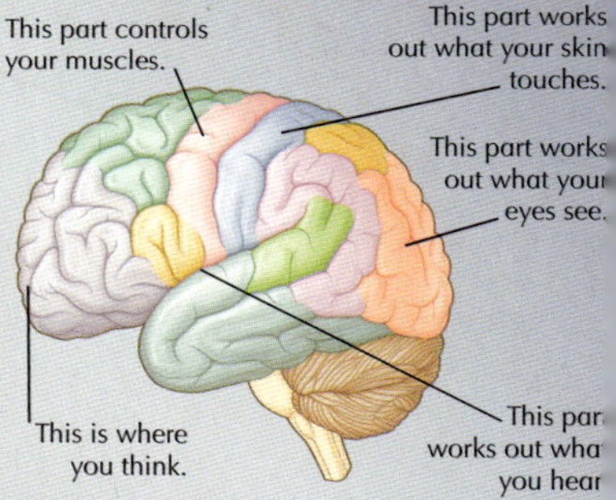

Brain parts

Different parts of your brain do different jobs. The brain also has two sides. The left side controls the right side of your body, and the right side controls the left side of your body.

Left-handed

Most people prefer to write or throw a ball with their right hand. We call them right-handed. But about one person in ten is left-handed. There are also more left-handed boys than girls.

Pain

When you hurt yourself, your nervous system sends messages to the brain to tell it you are in pain. The brain makes you feel pain to warn you that there's a problem.

Problem solving

To play a game like chess, you use your brain in lots of ways. You have to learn and remember how to move the pieces. Then you have to work out what will happen next when you make a move.

DID YOU KNOW?

As you grow up to become an adult, your body grows about 20 times bigger. But your brain only gets four times bigger.

Learning

To learn you need to remember things. Your brain can store and find things more quickly than the biggest computer. To play music you have to remember what the notes mean and where to put your fingers to play them.

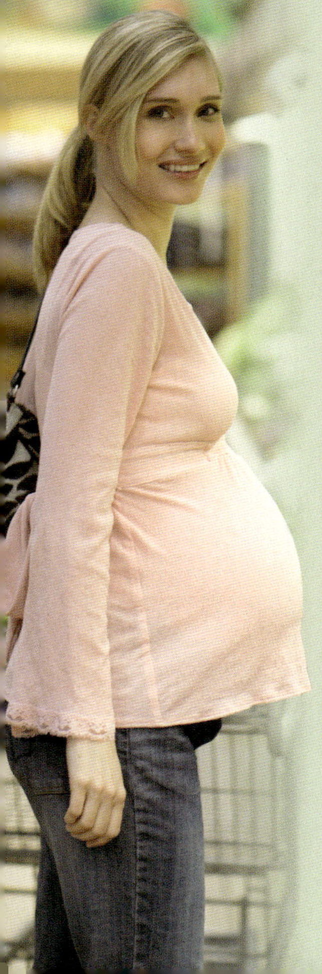

Babies and growing up

When a baby is born, we think that it has just started its life. But it has already been growing for nine months inside its mother. The baby grows into a child, then a teenager, and finally an adult.

Before birth

A baby starts its life as a tiny speck, as small as the dot on this "i." Over many weeks, its body takes shape. The baby grows inside its mother's body, in a special part called the womb.

Young children

Young children grow and learn very quickly. Most children can ride a bike, and read and write, by the time they are eight years old.

Adults

Today more people are living long and healthy lives. Women usually live longer than men, but lots of people live for 70 years or more. In 2006 the oldest person alive was 116-year-old Elizabeth Bolden from the USA.

Teenagers

Teenagers go through a stage known as puberty. This is when their bodies change to become more like those of adults. By the time they reach 20 they will stop growing.

Twins

When two babies are born at the same time we call them twins. Some twins are so similar in appearance that it can be hard to tell them apart. We call them identical twins.

Staying well

There are many ways you can stay fit and keep healthy. What you eat is very important. So are exercise and playing sports and games.

Exercise

Exercise is good for you. You can play games like skipping, catching, or football, or run, dance, or swim. Exercise keeps your heart fit and your muscles strong. Exercise even helps your brain. It can relax you and make you feel good.

Fresh food

The right kind of food is very important to keep your body healthy. Fresh vegetables and fruit are especially good for health because they are full of vitamins and minerals.

Keeping safe

Almost everything we do has risks. But we can stay safe by taking care. Always stop, look, and listen carefully before crossing a road. And if you are bicycling, skateboarding, or rollerblading, a helmet will protect you in case you fall over.

Too big

If you eat too much food, and do not exercise very much, you will get fat. Being overweight is bad for your heart and puts extra strain on your joints.

Sleep

Sleep allows your body to rest and your brain to sort out everything you have learned during the day. There are two kinds of sleep, deep sleep and light sleep. It is during light sleep that you dream.

DID YOU KNOW?

The number of hours you need to sleep gets smaller as you get older. Babies need up to 20 hours of sleep a day. Young children need about ten. Most adults sleep for seven or eight hours.

Doctors and medicines

Most people are well for most of the time. But sometimes people catch germs that make them feel ill. Or they can suffer an injury like a cut or bruise, or even a broken bone.

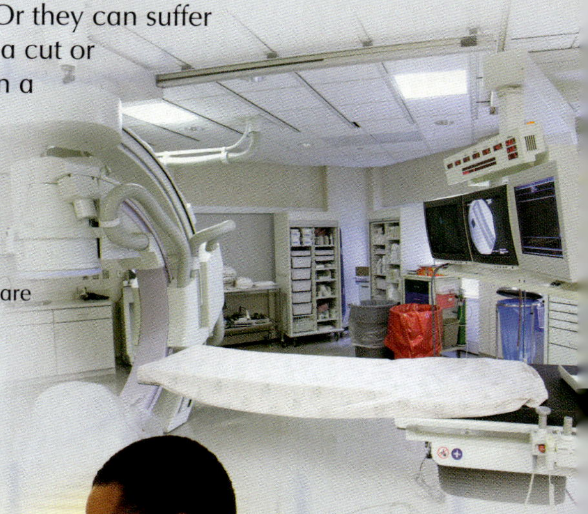

Hospital

Sometimes people have to go to the hospital. Doctors and nurses take care of them, helped by all kinds of machines and medicine. New ways to make us better are being discovered all the time.

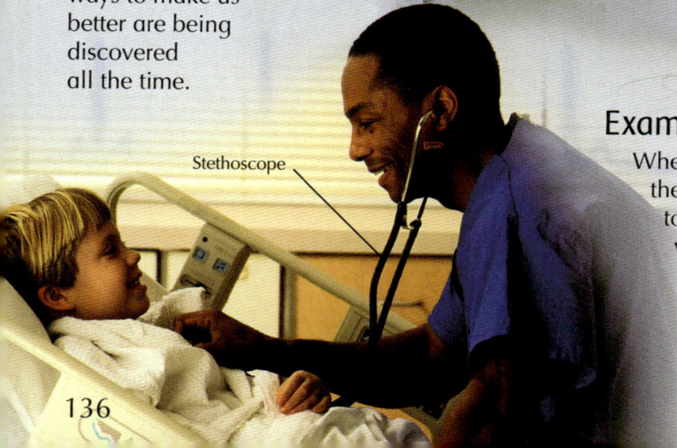

Examination

When you are sick, the doctor's job is to find out what is wrong with you. The doctor may listen to your heart using a stethoscope.

Medicines

There are lots of medicines for all kinds of illnesses. Some medicine can be bought from a drugstore or supermarket. Others may only be given, or prescribed, by a doctor.

Different doctors

Depending on what is wrong with us, there are lots of different doctors who can help. Some doctors will give us medicine. Others do operations or fix broken bones. Dentists take care of our teeth, and opticians look after our eyes.

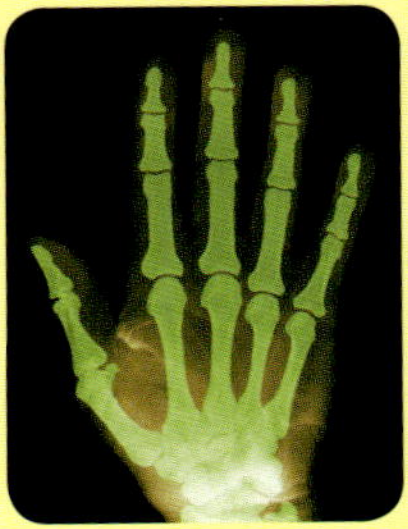

X-ray vision

With an X-ray machine doctors can see all the bones inside your body. This helps them see problems such as a broken bone or a damaged joint.

Hospitals have all kinds of doctors and nursing staff to help make sick people better.

Science

Science is about understanding the world around us. By finding out how animals and plants live and grow, scientists can help farmers produce more food, and doctors cure diseases. Scientists investigate what things are made of, too. This helps us make useful new materials. Scientists also study the stars and planets, the weather, and even the rocks that make up the Earth.

What is it made of?

Every substance, material, and object in the universe is made up of tiny particles called atoms. There are just over a hundred different kinds of atoms. Some substances, like gold, contain only one kind of atom, but others, such as plastic, contain atoms of several different kinds.

Too small to see

A microscope magnifies things (makes them look larger). You can use it to look at the dust-like pollen from a flower or the tiny grains of sand that make up a rock. But atoms are much too small to see, even with a microscope.

Building with atoms

Atoms are like the building blocks of the universe. Just as toy blocks can be clipped together to make different shapes, tiny atoms join together in different ways to make all the things we see around us—including our own bodies.

Blue, yellow, and red are called primary colors. You can use them to mix any color you like.

All mixed up

When you mix some substances together, you can't separate them again. For example, if you mix colored paints, you can't "unmix" them to get the original colors back.

Easy to separate

Some substances are easy to separate. If you add water to sand you get a squishy mixture. But when sand dries out, you are left with just sand again.

Clothes up close

Your clothes are made up of tiny threads, or fibers, which you can see magnified here. Some are natural fibers, like wool and cotton. Others, like nylon, are made from chemicals in factories.

Energy

Energy is the ability to make things happen, move, or change. There are many kinds of energy, including light, heat, electricity, and sound. One kind of energy can also change into another.

Energy for life

You need energy to run, jump, shout, breathe, and even think. All your energy comes from the food you eat. Your stomach breaks down the food to unlock the energy stored inside it.

Energy from the Sun

Heat from the Sun warms the air, land, and sea. Plants use the energy in sunlight to make their own food. Sunlight can also be turned into electricity using solar panels.

This car has solar panels that make electricity to drive its wheels.

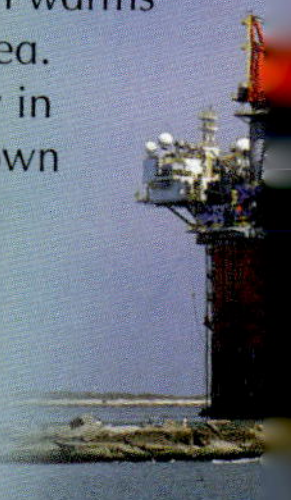

Food energy

Sugary foods gives us instant energy. Starchy foods, such as pasta, bread, and rice, release their energy more slowly, and keep us going for a longer time.

Movement energy

Things that move very fast, such as the wind, have a lot of energy. A wind turbine has propeller-like blades that turn in the wind. The turning blades drive a generator that produces electricity.

Fuel energy

Fuels are energy-rich substances that we burn for light and heat, and to power machinery. Coal, oil, and gas are called fossil fuels. They formed millions of years ago from the remains of dead plants and animals.

An oil rig pumps oil from under the ocean floor.

DID YOU KNOW?

The Sun's energy makes life on Earth possible. Heat and light take just over eight minutes to travel from the Sun's surface to the Earth.

Solid, liquid, gas

Substances can exist in three different forms. Solids keep their shape and size. Liquids can flow and change shape, but they can't be squeezed smaller. Gases can flow and change shape. They can also be squeezed smaller or spread out bigger.

Different water

Liquid water flows in rivers and oceans. Water also exists as solid ice, and as a gas called steam.

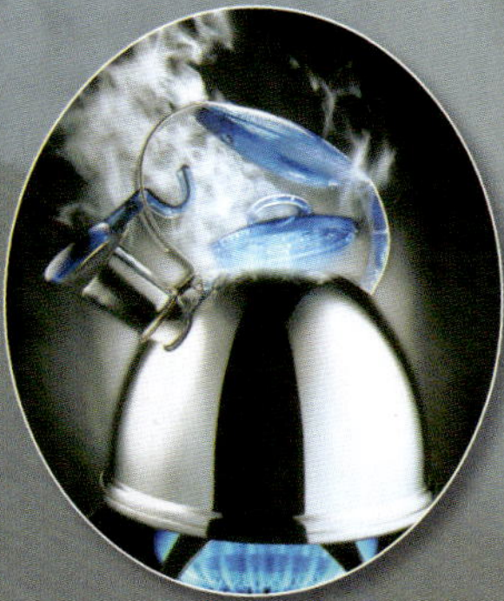

From water to steam

When we heat water in a saucepan, bubbles of gas form in the water and escape as steam. The change from a liquid into a gas is called evaporation. When a gas cools and turns back into a liquid, this is called condensation.

Floating on air

Air is a mixture of gases, such as nitrogen, oxygen, and carbon dioxide. Some gases weigh less than the gases in air. This blimp is filled with a gas called helium. Helium is lighter than air, so the blimp floats.

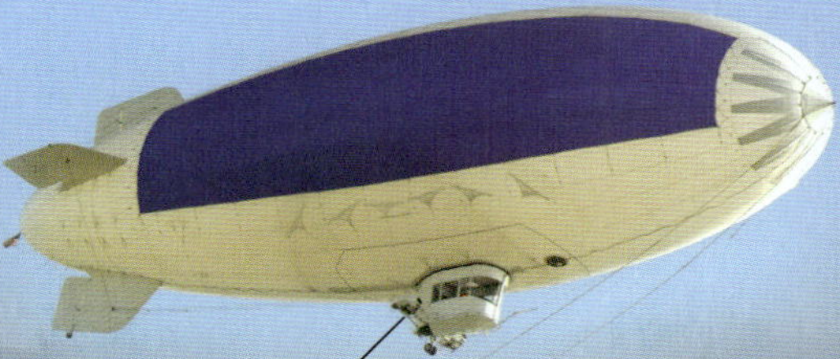

Blimps, also called airships, only need small engines because they are so light.

DID YOU KNOW?

If you squeeze a gas smaller, it gets hotter. This is why a bicycle pump becomes warm when you pump up a tire.

Melt and freeze

If a solid is heated enough it will turn into a liquid. This is called melting. A glass-blower makes vases by blowing air into melted glass. When the glass cools, it becomes solid again.

This glass is so hot it glows red. Heat makes it soft so it can be shaped.

Hot and cold

We use the word temperature to talk about how hot or cold something is. As an object gets warmer, its temperature rises. As it gets cooler, its temperature falls.

Keeping warm

People who live in cold places wear several layers of thick clothing. Air trapped between the layers helps stop their bodies losing heat to the air.

Traveling heat

Heat travels out from a campfire through the air to warm our bodies. Heat can travel through solid materials, too. When you put your hands around a cup of hot chocolate, you can feel the warmth of the drink it contains.

Temperature scale

We measure how hot an object is with a thermometer. This has a temperature scale divided into units called degrees, usually degrees Fahrenheit (°F) or degrees Celsius (°C). A hot day is about 90°F. An ice cream is about 32°F—this is why it cools you down.

An ice cream helps you cool off on a hot day.

What temperature is it?

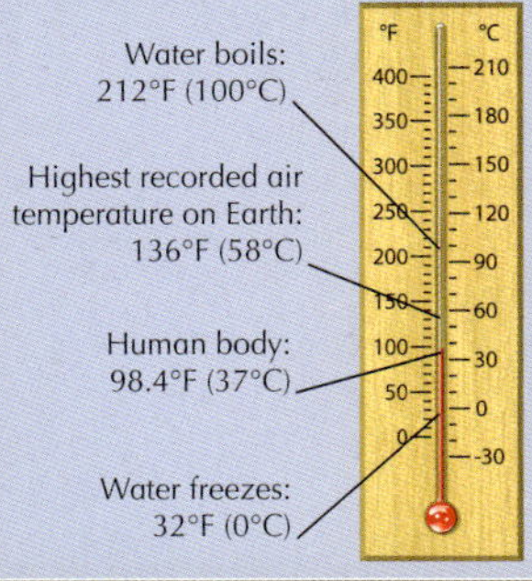

Desert extremes

By day, deserts are scorched by the burning sunshine. At night, because there is no cloud cover, temperatures can plunge to below freezing.

Light and color

We can see objects because light bounces, or reflects, off them and enters our eyes. The most important light source is the Sun. Sunlight looks white, but it is really made up of many different colors. Objects look colored because they only reflect some of the colors in sunlight.

DID YOU KNOW?

We often say there are seven colors in the rainbow: red, orange, yellow, green, blue, indigo, and violet. But these are just the most obvious ones. In fact, a rainbow contains millions of different colors.

Single rainbows are always red on the outside, or top, of their arc.

Rainbow colors

When the sun comes out during a shower of rain, you might see a rainbow. As sunlight shines through small drops of rain in the sky, the raindrops split the white sunlight into its many colors.

Making our own light

At night and in dark places such as caves, we have to make our own light. In the past, people used candles, fires, and oil lamps to see in the dark. Now we have electric lightbulbs in our homes, electric street lights, and battery-powered flashlights.

Color changers

Colored lights can change the way something looks to us. Even though we know that a banana is yellow, under a blue light it reflects the light's color and looks blue.

Mirror image

Smooth, shiny surfaces reflect light best of all. When you look into a mirror, a window, or the surface of calm water, you can see an image of yourself. This is called a reflection. This polar bear is investigating its reflection in the water.

Sound

Sounds are made when objects move rapidly to and fro. This shaking movement is called vibration. Vibrations travel through the air like ripples through water. We hear sounds with our ears.

Making music

Musical instruments have parts that vibrate to make sound. The strings of a guitar vibrate when you pluck them, and the skin on top of a drum vibrates when you hit it. When you blow into a recorder, the air inside it vibrates.

Animal sounds

When you talk, you make sound inside your throat. Many animals make sounds in their throats, too. A leopard roars as a warning. A baby bird chirps to tell its parents it's hungry.

Loud and soft

The harder you bang a drum, the louder the sound it makes. If a sound is too loud it can damage your ears. This is why people who work with noisy machines wear ear covers to protect their hearing.

High and low

Some sounds are high or shrill, like a bird singing. We say that they have a high pitch. Other sounds are low and rumbling, like the boom of thunder. These sounds have a low pitch.

A pan flute has long tubes for low notes, and short ones for high notes.

Forces

A force is a push or a pull. When forces act in different directions, they can make an object move, stop, or change direction. They can also squeeze, squash, stretch, bend, or twist an object to change its shape.

Riding force

You need force to ride a bicycle. The force of your feet pushing on the pedals pulls the chain around and turns the rear wheel. Your hands pull on the brake levers, while your arms pull on the handlebars to steer.

Balanced forces

Sometimes two forces can balance each other. If two tug-of-war teams pull on the rope with the same force, neither one will move. In the end, usually one side gets weaker and is pulled along by the stronger team.

Scary force

As a rollercoaster races around a track doing loop-the-loop, a force keeps people pressed into their seats, like an invisible safety belt. This force is called centripetal force.

DID YOU KNOW?

A space rocket blasts off with 10 million times as much force as a family car going along the street.

Slowing force

A force called friction tries to slow down objects that slide past each other. There is less friction between smooth surfaces than rough ones. This is why it is easier to sled over smooth, slidy snow than over rough gravel.

Down to Earth

People often wish they could fly like birds. But we are kept on the ground by the Earth's gravity. This is a downward force that pulls on everything—even birds, which is why they must flap their wings to stay in the air.

Falling fast

When skydivers jump out of a plane, they fall very fast. This is because gravity pulls them down to the ground. When their parachutes open, they catch the air, so the skydivers fall more slowly.

Beating gravity

As a plane moves along the runway, the air rushing over its wings makes an upward force called lift. When lift is greater than the force of gravity, the plane takes off.

Earth's gravity

Everything has gravity—including you! You pull on the Earth, just as the Earth pulls on you. But gravity depends on size. You are quite small, so your gravity is weak. The Earth is huge, so it has very strong gravity.

Away from the Earth's gravity, out in space, everything floats as if it were weightless.

DID YOU KNOW?

A rocket has to reach a certain speed to break free of the Earth's gravity and get into space. This speed is called "escape velocity." It is 300 times faster than a car speeding along a highway!

Sliding down

The force of gravity is at work in the playground too. It's gravity that pulls you down a slide. The steeper the slide, the faster you go.

Floating and sinking

A huge steel ship, such as a cruiseliner, resembles a small mountain. But why does the ship float, when the mountain would sink? The answer lies in the shape of the ship and the fact that it is full of air.

Big but hollow

A mountain is solid rock. But a big ship isn't solid metal. It has a huge hull filled mostly with air. This large, hollow shape makes the ship light for its size, and allows it to float. This is known as buoyancy.

Rubber ring

Air-filled armbands and rings work a little like a ship's hull. They also make you much bigger in the water, with hardly any extra weight.

Floating air

The air inside a balloon is heated by a gas burner. The hot air is lighter than the cold air outside, so the balloon floats.

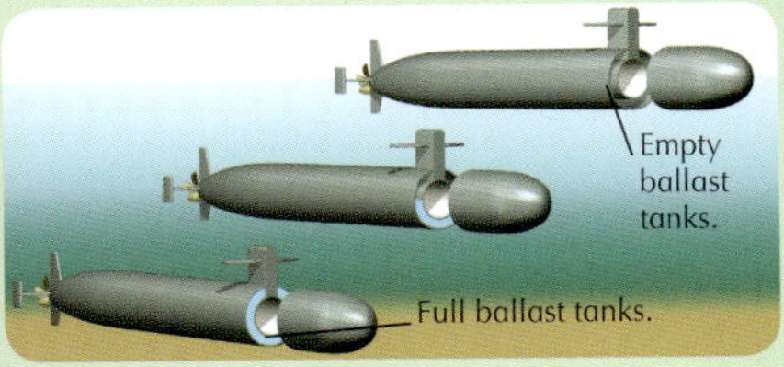

Diving and surfacing

A submarine has ballast tanks to help it to dive under water and rise to the surface. Filling the tanks with water makes the submarine heavier, so it sinks. Pumping air into the tanks makes the submarine lighter, so it floats.

Floating bottle

It's the air trapped in this glass bottle that keeps the bottle afloat. If the cork comes out and the bottle fills with water, it will sink.

Electricity

Electricity is a kind of energy that flows through wires. We use electricity to give us light and heat, and to make machines work. Electricity can also be dangerous—it can even kill.

Skilled work

People who make and mend electrical machines are called electricians and electrical engineers. They understand how to work safely with electricity.

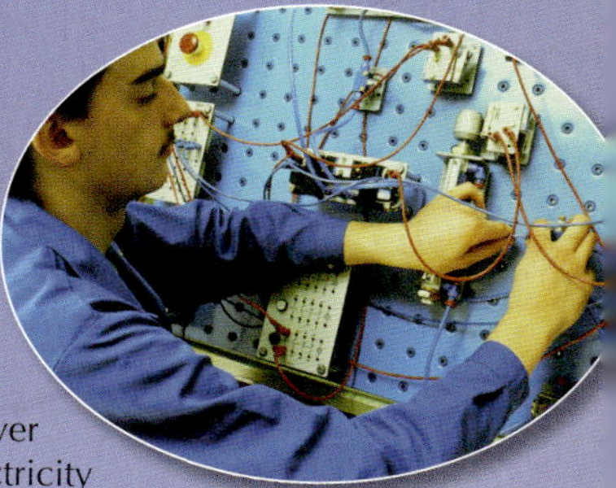

Power station

Most of the electricity used in homes, factories, and offices is produced in power stations. The electricity flows along thick cables (wires) carried underground or by tall towers called pylons.

How electricity is made

1. Most power stations make electricity from fuels, such as gas, oil, or coal.

2. The gas, oil, or coal is burned to produce steam. The steam is used to drive generators.

3. The generators make electricity, which is carried by cables to our homes and factories.

4. In our homes we use electricity for heat, light, cooking, and watching TV.

Battery power

Batteries are small supplies of electricity that you can carry around. Inside them are chemicals that work together to produce electricity. Batteries power things such as portable game consoles and flashlights.

Switched on

Electricity is so useful because it can travel from place to place along wires, and we can switch it on and off. It can power tools such as drills, sanders, and saws.

Welders use the heat from a spark of electricity to join metals together.

Magnets

A magnet creates a special force called magnetism. Magnets can attract (pull toward) and repel (push away) each other. They also attract some metals.

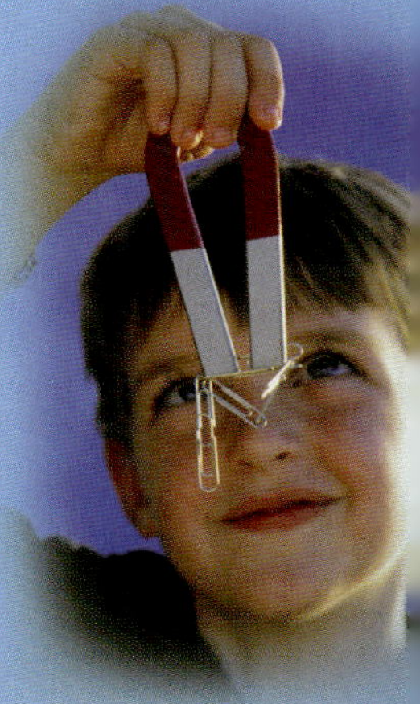

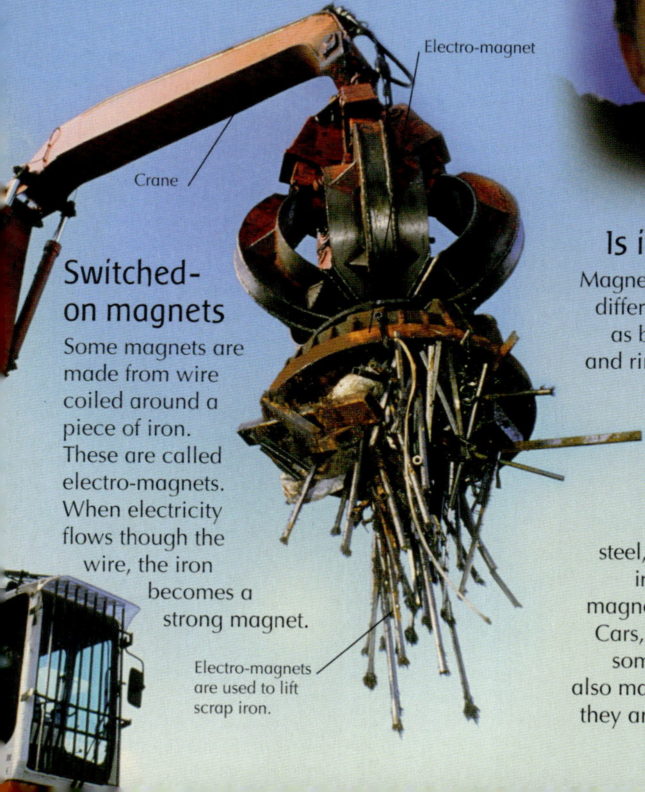

Electro-magnets are used to lift scrap iron.

Switched-on magnets

Some magnets are made from wire coiled around a piece of iron. These are called electro-magnets. When electricity flows though the wire, the iron becomes a strong magnet.

Is it magnetic?

Magnets come in many different shapes, such as bars, horseshoes, and rings. All magnets attract the metal iron, so we say that iron is "magnetic." A refrigerator door is made of steel, which is mostly iron. That is why a magnet will stick to it. Cars, paperclips, and some food cans are also magnetic, because they are made of steel.

Giant magnet

The whole Earth is like a giant magnet. Because of this we can find our way using a magnetic compass. This has a magnetized needle that always lines up to point north-south.

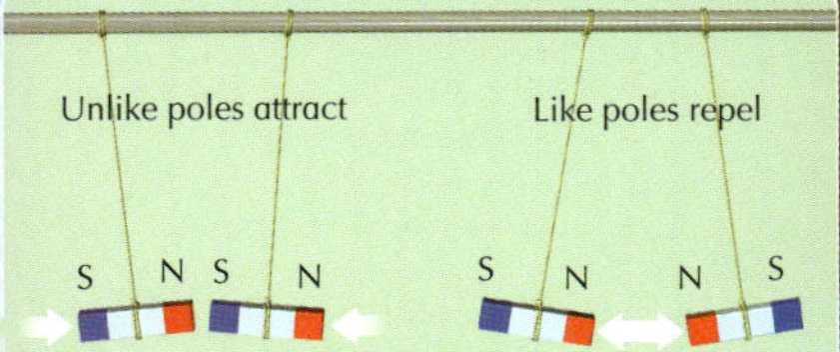

Attract or repel?

A magnet's magnetism is strongest at two ends, known as its north pole (N) and its south pole (S). If two magnets are placed with different poles facing each other, they will pull together. If two poles of the same kind are lined up, they will push apart.

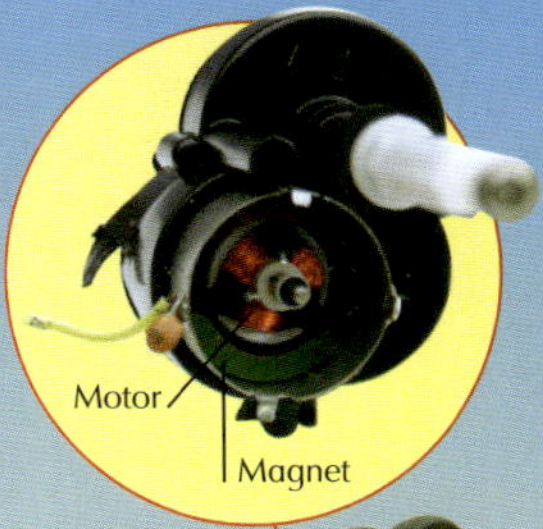

Magnets everywhere

Every day we use magnets without knowing. Anything with an electric motor, such as this remote-controlled model car, has magnets inside the motor. The electricity and magnetism work together to make the motor turn.

Materials

Choosing the right material for a job is very important. If you want a cup to drink out of, it has to be waterproof. If you want to build a house, you have to choose materials that are strong, like bricks or steel.

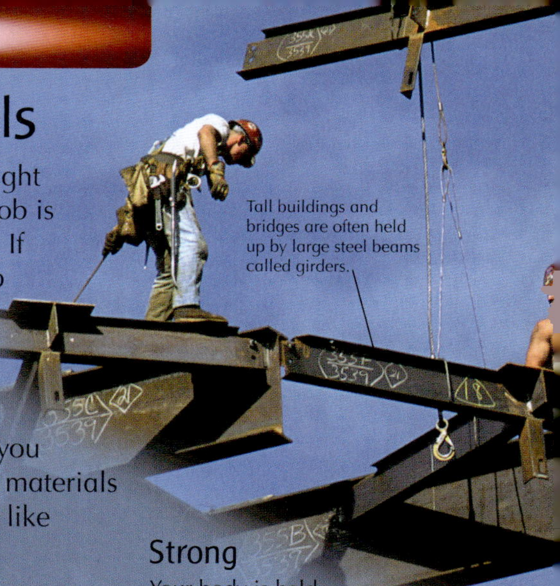

Tall buildings and bridges are often held up by large steel beams called girders.

Strong

Your body is held up by a skeleton of strong bones. A skyscraper has a skeleton of long beams, made of the metal called steel. Steel is strong enough to hold the building up without bending or breaking.

Squashy and stretchy

Some materials, such as a sponge or a bouncy trampoline, can be squashed or stretched. When you let go, they will quickly spring back into shape.

Tough and colorful

There are hundreds of different plastics. Plastic is a very useful material, because it can be molded into any shape. It also lasts for a long time and isn't harmed by the weather. This is why it is often used to make playground equipment.

Baked hard

Pots, plates, and cups are made from materials called ceramics. These materials are shaped while they are soft and floppy. Then they are baked in an oven to make them hard.

DID YOU KNOW?

Many materials can be recycled, or used again. They include glass, metal, paper, and plastic. This helps the environment because less trash ends up in garbage dumps.

Machines and gadgets

We build machines and gadgets to help us do things. Some machines, like a bottle-opener, are quite simple. Others, like a jumbo jet, which has over six million parts, are amazingly complicated. Some machines, like jet skis, only really help us enjoy ourselves! Gadgets are usually little devices that do something to help you. Many gadgets, such as cell phones, can be both useful and a lot of fun.

Simple machines

Machines make it easier for us to do things, or help us do things we could not do at all. Some of the most useful machines, like ramps, levers, and wheels, are also really simple.

Ramps

Ramps are sometimes used instead of stairs or escalators. They help people move from one level to another. They are useful for people with wheelchairs or luggage.

Gears

Gears are the toothed wheels that your bicycle chain wraps around. Usually there is one big gear wheel attached to the pedals, and one or more smaller gear wheels attached to the back wheel. Having gears of different sizes at the back makes it easier for you to ride your bicycle up and down hills.

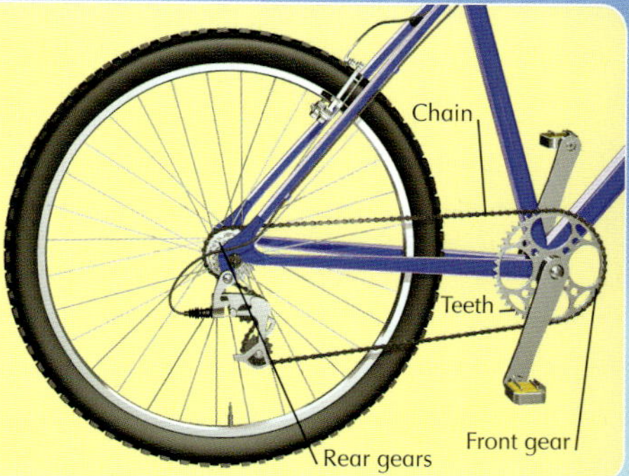

Wheels

Wheels help us move or carry heavy loads. Some wheels are tiny. Others are over 10 feet high. Bigger wheels make it easier for heavy trucks to travel over rough ground without getting stuck in the mud.

Screws and propellers

The screw is a simple machine. As you turn a wood screw with a screwdriver it pulls its way into the wood. A ship's propeller is also a kind of screw. But it pushes, instead of pulls, the ship through the water.

Levers

A lever can help us lift things that would usually be too heavy for us. The seesaw is a lever that allows you to lift your partner into the air.

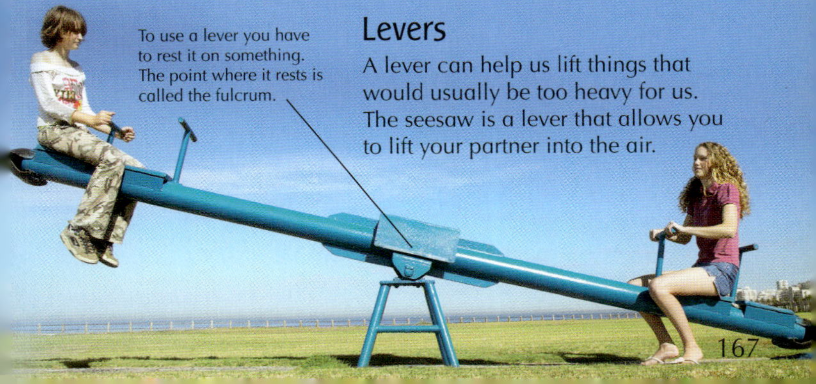

To use a lever you have to rest it on something. The point where it rests is called the fulcrum.

In the home

Kitchens have lots of machines and gadgets. They help us prepare and cook our food. We also use machines to keep our house and clothes clean. Most machines are powered by electricity.

Vacuum cleaners

Vacuum cleaners use an electric motor to create powerful suction. The suction pulls the dirt and dust into the cleaner.

Washing machines

Washing machines have a large drum that is turned by a big electric motor. Holes in the drum let the water in and out to wash the clothes. When it is washing, the drum turns backward and forward quite slowly.

DID YOU KNOW?

Over 100 years ago there was no electricity. People worked all their machines by hand. Imagine life without a washing machine and vacuum cleaner.

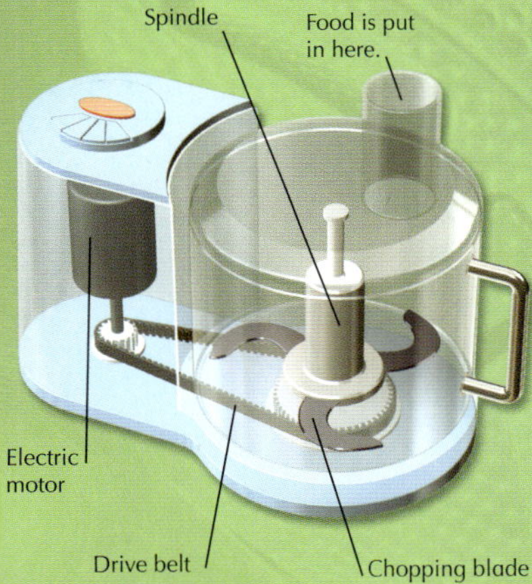

Food processors

Food processors can prepare vegetables or mix ingredients much faster than you can do by hand. They have an electric motor that turns a spindle very fast. Sharp blades, for chopping, or whisks, for mixing, can then be fitted to the spindle.

Two in one

A manual can-opener is two machines in one. The lever part pushes the blade onto the can. The blade cuts a long hole around the top of the can.

High-speed juicers

Juicers have very powerful motors. Blades chop and shred the fruit or vegetables into a soft mushy mixture called pulp. The pulp is then pushed through a sieve to squeeze out all the juice.

Tools for the job

Whatever the job, from drilling a hole to making a baseball bat, there is a tool that is made to do it. Many tools are powered by electric motors, but a few still need muscle power.

Flying sparks

A grinder has a hard spinning disk that can be used to smooth, shape, or cut things. When it grinds metal, sparks and sharp pieces of metal fly in all directions.

Lathes

A lathe is a special machine for making shapes out of wood or metal. Baseball bats, candlesticks, and bolts can be made with a lathe. To make a bat, the wood is held at one end of the lathe and spun around. A cutting tool is then held against the wood to shape it.

Inside an electric drill

An electric drill has a powerful motor inside. The drill "bit" is the part that makes the hole. It has a sharp tip and a spiral groove to carry away the material being drilled off. The bit is held tightly in metal jaws called the chuck.

DID YOU KNOW?

The fastest drills can spin around more than 1,000 times every second. That is 60,000 times a minute!

Small but sharp

A saw has small, sharp teeth. The teeth are bent alternately to each side, first one way, then the other. This makes the saw cut a wide slot, and stops it getting stuck.

On the farm

Farms once employed lots of people to work on the land and look after the animals. Today big machines do many of the jobs people once did. And as farms have become bigger, so have the machines.

Plowing time

Plows are like big curved shovels that dig and turn over the soil at the same time. They are pulled by big tractors with powerful engines. Plowing helps bury weeds and let air into the soil.

Milking machine

When cows were milked by hand, the job used to take all morning. Today milking machines can milk a whole herd of cows in less than an hour.

Spraying apples

Helicopters and airplanes are sometimes used to spray crops to keep them healthy. But many farmers are trying not to use so many chemicals and to grow crops more naturally. This is called organic farming.

Combine harvester

A combine harvester does several jobs. First it cuts the wheat. Then it "threshes" it to separate the grain from the waste straw. The waste is thrown out the back as the combine moves along. The grain is stored until it can be unloaded, when it is pushed through a long tube into a trailer.

In the factory

A factory is a big building filled with machines. Some factories are used for making things, such as paper or metal. In other factories, things are put together, such as cars or computers.

Faster and faster

New ideas and better machines mean that factories can make more things each year, and make them faster. Some factories make five million bottles of drink every day.

Robot welding machine

Robots

A robot is a machine that can do a job or task all by itself. But it still needs a person to tell it how to do the job the first time. Once a robot knows how to do something, it will do it exactly the same way every time. And it doesn't get tired like people!

Assembly line

On an assembly line lots of workers or machines each do a part of a job. They each help to put together, or "assemble," things that move along beside them on a conveyor belt. At the end of the line, the product is complete.

Printing press

Newspapers, magazines, and books are printed on huge machines called presses. The paper is fed into the presses from enormous rolls.

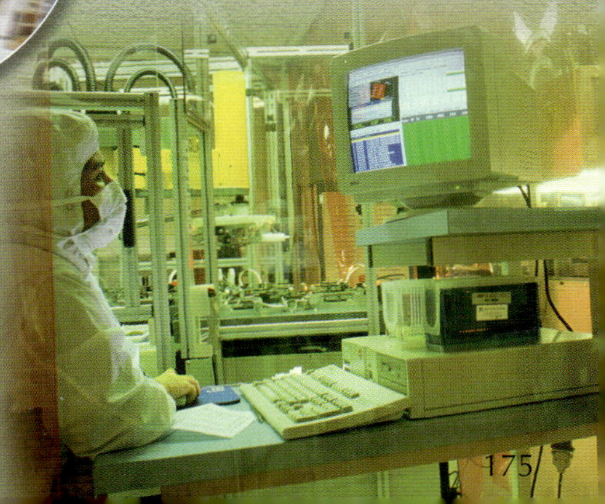

Super clean

Computers have tiny parts that must be kept free of dirt or dust. Computer factories are often as clean as hospitals. The workers even wear hats and masks.

At the building site

Long ago, people put up buildings using their own muscles and a few simple tools. Today a building site is full of huge, powerful machines. With their help, a tall skyscraper can be built in just three months.

Lifting

A tower crane lifts heavy loads around the building site. As the building gets taller, extra parts have to be added to the crane's tower, so it gets taller, too.

Flattening

A bulldozer uses its big blade to push huge piles of soil and flatten the ground. It moves along slowly on big metal caterpillar tracks.

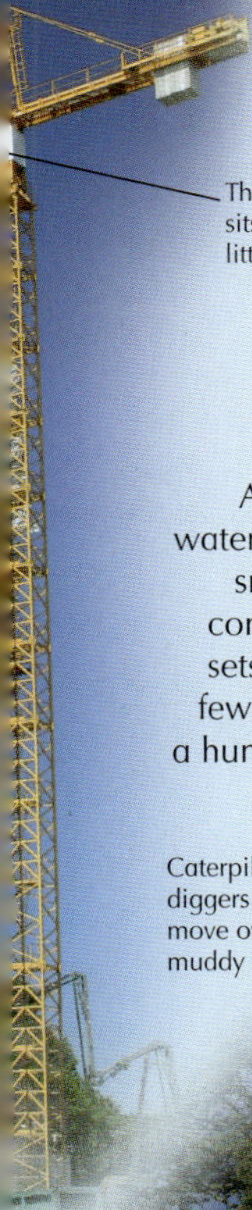

The crane operator sits high up in a little cabin.

Mixing

A mixer stirs together water, cement, sand, and small stones to make concrete. The concrete sets, or goes hard, in a few hours, and lasts for a hundred years or more.

Caterpillar tracks help diggers and bulldozers move over rough or muddy ground.

Excavator

An excavator, also called a 360, digs holes in the ground. These are filled with concrete to form the base of a building. It also digs trenches for pipes and wires, and fills them in again afterward.

On the road

Our roads are busy with machines we call vehicles. There are cars, motorcycles, trucks, and buses. They take people, loads, and cargo from one place to another.

This electric car is not only quiet and clean, it also goes very fast.

Electric cars

Most cars have gas or diesel engines. An electric car has big batteries that power an electric motor. It is quiet and wastes less energy than a gas-engined car.

Bendy buses

Bendy buses are like two buses joined together. They can carry more people around crowded cities—and they only need one driver.

On two wheels

A motorcycle is small and fast. But it can only carry one or two people. Some racing cycles can travel at over 180 miles an hour.

DID YOU KNOW?

There are around a billion cars in the world. Ten new ones are made every second.

Tractor-trailer trucks

The biggest trucks are articulated, which means that they have a separate cab and engine at the front, called a tractor, and a big load-carrying trailer at the back.

Going by train

Trains run on metal railway lines called tracks. Passenger trains stop at stations so people can get on and off. Freight trains carry all kinds of loads, from coal and sand, to mail and cars.

Bullet trains

Japan has some of the fastest trains in the world. Known as "bullet trains," they can travel at speeds of nearly 185 miles an hour.

Signals and points

Where a road crosses a railway line, there is usually a barrier and lights to warn drivers when a train is coming. Trains can change onto a different track at special places called "points." The rails slide sideways to join another line and make the train change direction.

Only one rail

Trains that have just one rail in the middle are called monorails. These trains are usually found in cities, airports, and docks.

DID YOU KNOW?

Trains called maglevs use magnetism to float above, and glide along, a single track. Some maglevs can go faster than 300 miles an hour.

Overhead wires

Some electric trains have motors at both ends, and even in the middle. These motors get their electricity from overhead wires that the train touches as it travels along.

In the air

The quickest way to travel a long way is to fly. In less than a day you can fly to the other side of the world. You begin and end your flight at an airport where the planes take off and land.

Lots of people

The biggest jumbo jets carry more than 500 people, as well as all their luggage. They can also carry enough fuel to fly halfway around the world without stopping.

Hover

Helicopters can take off and land without a runway. They can also "hover," or stay still in one place, in the sky. This makes them useful for all kinds of jobs, including firefighting and rescuing people from the sea.

This Fire Department helicopter is dropping water on a forest fire.

Skillful flying

Display pilots fly their planes very close together and do tricks such as spinning and flying upside down. They also fly big circles called "looping the loop."

The display team of the U.S. Navy is called the Blue Angels.

The Airbus A380 is the largest passenger plane in the world. It can carry up to 840 passengers.

How wings work

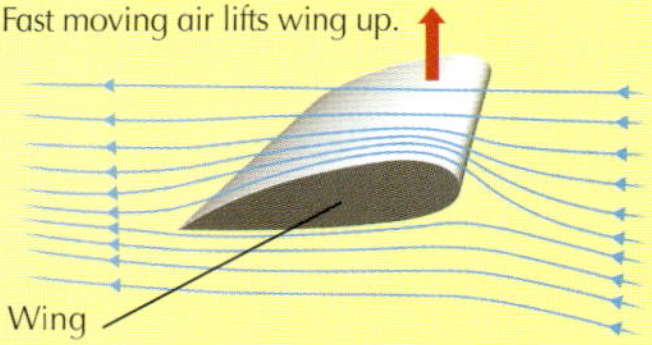

To take off, a plane has to speed along the runway. As it moves, the teardrop shape of its wings forces air to move faster over the top of the wing than under it. This creates suction above the wing that lifts the plane up into the air.

At the controls

The pilot flies the plane from the cockpit. In the cockpit of a big passenger plane there are hundreds of dials, lights, screens, and controls. A powerful computer called the "automatic pilot" helps the pilot to fly the plane safely.

On the ocean

On the ocean, ships and boats must travel carefully. There are no signs to follow and the weather can make the water rough and dangerous. Ships use radios or satellites in space to guide them.

Jet skis

Jet skis are like jet-powered motorcycles you ride on water. They have powerful engines that suck in water and then squirt it out behind in a powerful jet. This pushes the jet ski along at high speed.

DID YOU KNOW?

Frenchman Bruno Peyron holds the record for the fastest anyone has ever sailed around the world. He did it in just over 50 days.

Supertankers

The largest boats ever built are called supertankers. They carry oil across the great oceans of the world. They are so big that they take 20 minutes to stop and need about 1¼ miles of open water to turn around in.

At high speed the hydrofoil rises out of the water.

Hydrofoils

Hydrofoils are boats that can rise up out of the water on special wings called foils. When moving slowly the hydrofoil looks like an ordinary boat. But as it goes faster it rises up onto its foils. It can then go even faster.

Blown along

Sailboats are blown along by the wind. If the wind is very strong the sailboat sometimes leans right over. As the wind changes direction, the people or "crew" pull ropes to change the direction of the sails to catch the wind.

This large sail is called a spinnaker.

Having fun

Many exciting machines are found at carnivals and amusement parks. They make us shout and scream with excitement and fear, but really we know that we are safe.

Spinning slowly

The Ferris wheel turns slowly and steadily. The cars tilt using hinges, so they always swing upright, even when they are at the top.

DID YOU KNOW?

The biggest Ferris wheel in the world is in Japan. It is 330 feet tall, carries 380 people, and takes 16 minutes to go around.

High speed thrills

Most rollercoasters have gears underneath the cars that fit into a row of teeth in the track. These pull the cars to the top of the ride. The higher they go, the faster they come down.

Indoor skydiving

An indoor skydiving machine uses an incredibly powerful fan to blast air up through a vent in the floor. You can experience the thrill of flying while only 4 feet above the ground.

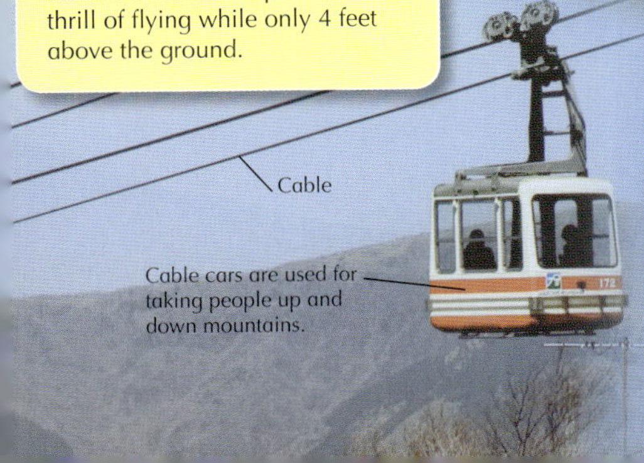

Cable cars are used for taking people up and down mountains.

Pulling along

The cable car hangs from a thick wire, or cable, in one long loop that goes around and around. It is turned at each end by wheels called pulleys.

Portable music players are sometimes called MP3 players.

Electronic gadgets

Gadgets are little machines that usually do something useful or fun. These days most gadgets are electronic, like portable music players, clever cell phones, or computer-controlled toys.

Portable music

Portable music players allow you to listen to music anywhere. By first compressing, or squashing, the music on a computer, you can squeeze lots of songs onto even the tiniest of portable players.

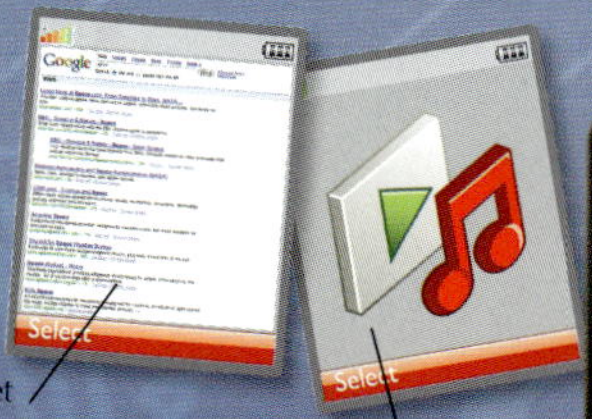

Cell phones

Some cell phones now do much more than just let you make telephone calls or send text messages. They can receive TV programs, take pictures, play music, and even surf the Internet.

High-tech toys

Many modern toys are packed with technology. This robot has a computer for a brain. It can be controlled without wires and can even "see" where it is going using special sensors for eyes.

Game machines

Some portable game consoles can do more than just play great games. They can also play music and show movies.

The computer

You can do so many things on a computer. It is possible to do simple things like write a story, but you can also store music and photos, watch a DVD, or find things out on the Internet.

Space

The world where we live is called planet Earth. It is huge. To walk around it without stopping would take you two years. But if you were far away in space, the Earth would look like a small blue disk the size of this "o." The Earth is one of a group of planets that circle a star we call the Sun. It is the light and warmth from the Sun that has helped life develop on Earth. So far we have not managed to find life anywhere else.

Solar system

The Earth is one of a group of planets that circle around the Sun. There are eight large planets, and a number of smaller ones—including Pluto. Together they are part of what is called the solar system.

The Sun

The Sun is the star at the center of our solar system. It is a huge ball of burning gas, about a million times bigger than the Earth. Without its heat and light, there would be no life on Earth.

The planets

All the planets travel around the Sun. The paths they follow are called orbits. Some orbits are round, others are slightly egg-shaped. The Earth takes a year to go right around the Sun. Mercury, which is much closer, only takes 87 days. Eris is so far away from the Sun that it takes 557 years to go all the way around.

Comet tails

A comet is a chunk of ice and dust. When it passes near the Sun, some of its ice turns to gas and forms a long tail that glows in the night sky. In 1996 the probe *Ulysses* found that the tail of comet Hyakutake was 350 million miles long.

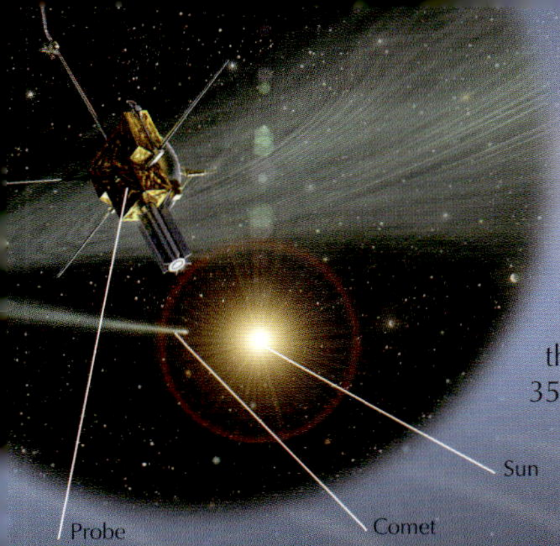

Exploring the night sky

Many of the planets in the solar system can be seen in the night sky. To your eyes they look just like bright stars. But if you look through a pair of binoculars, or a telescope, they appear like tiny discs. You may even be able to see Saturn's rings.

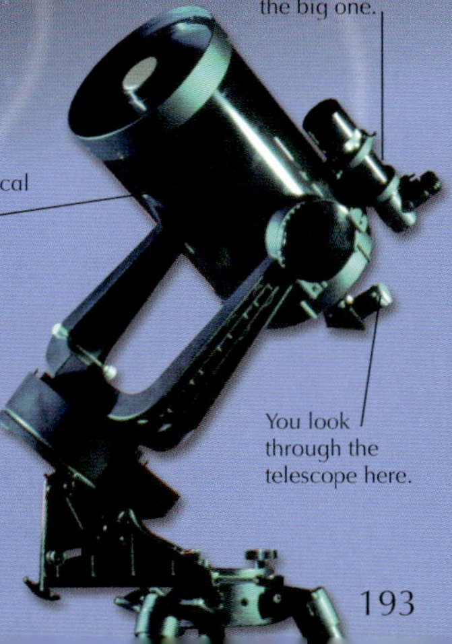

The Moon

A moon is a big ball of rock that goes around a planet. Most of the planets in the solar system have moons. Jupiter has over 60! But the Earth has just one.

The Moon's surface

The Moon's surface is made up of hills and dusty plains, known as seas. Everywhere there are bowl-shaped holes called craters. These were made when huge rocks, or meteors, crashed into the Moon.

Why the Moon changes shape

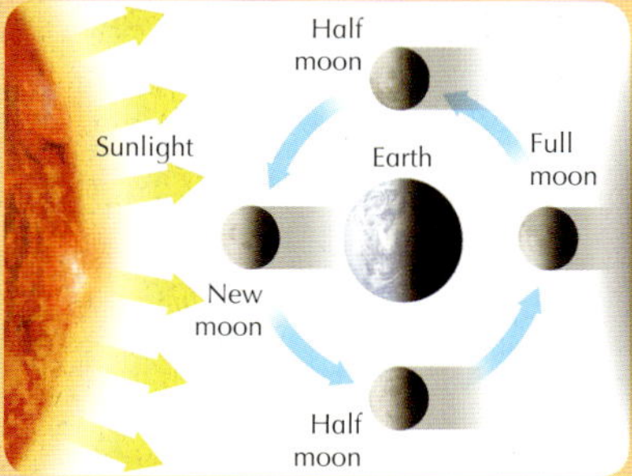

The Moon shines because it reflects the light of the Sun that shines on it. As the Moon moves around the Earth it seems to change shape, because we only see the part of it lit by the Sun. When the Moon is between the Earth and the Sun, you can't see it. This is called a new moon.

This dark area is called a sea.

DID YOU KNOW?

The Moon is much smaller than the Earth. You could fit 50 Moons inside the Earth.

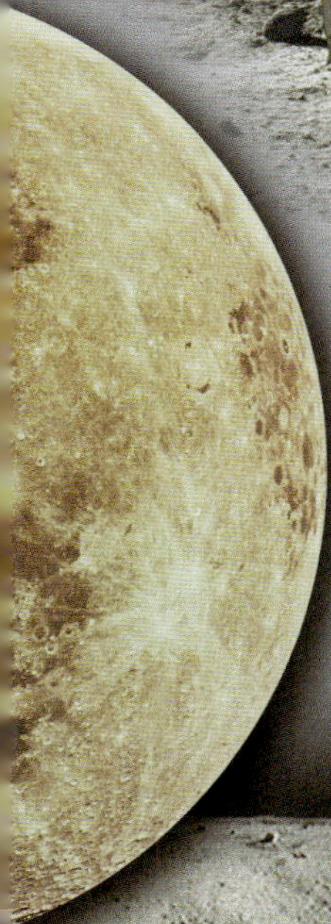

Less gravity

The Moon is dry and rocky. It has no air to breathe. Because it has less gravity, you could jump six times higher on the Moon than you could on Earth.

Moon landing

Only 12 people have ever walked on the Moon. Astronaut Neil Armstrong was the first when he stepped onto the Moon in 1969. He flew there in a spacecraft called *Apollo 11*.

The Sun

When we look into the night sky we see lots of tiny twinkling stars. During the day, a much bigger star gives our world light and heat. This is the Sun. It seems so huge because it is much closer to the Earth than any other star.

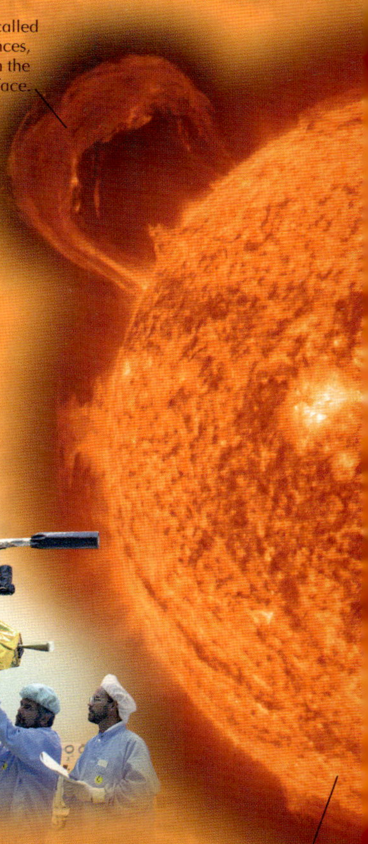

Flames, called prominences, leap from the Sun's surface.

At 10,000°F, the Sun is 30 times hotter than a kitchen oven.

Studying the Sun

This spacecraft, called *Ulysses*, was launched in 1990 to study the Sun. It is still out in space, telling us more about the Sun every day.

Solar eclipse

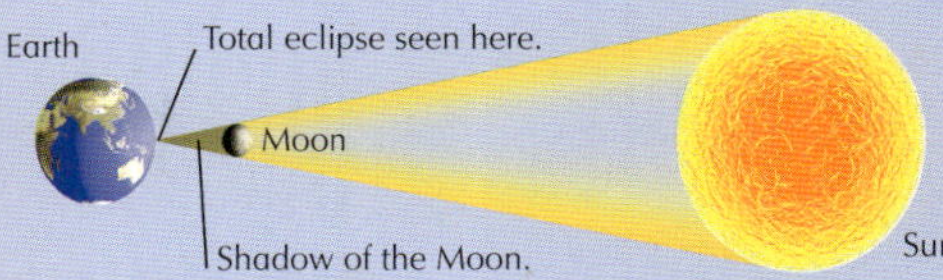

Sometimes the Moon moves in front of the Sun during the day. When it blots out all the Sun's light we call it a total eclipse. When it just covers part of the Sun, we call it a partial eclipse.

Total eclipse

Too bright

You should never look directly at the Sun. It is so bright it would damage your eyes. To look at an eclipse you need to wear special glasses. Scientists look at the Sun by projecting its image onto a screen.

The Sun is made up of the gases hydrogen and helium.

The rocky planets

The nearest planet to us is Venus. Mars and Mercury are also quite close. Like the Earth, these planets are huge balls of rock, but they are all smaller than the Earth.

DID YOU KNOW?

When astronomers first studied Mars, they thought they could see canals on its surface. But when the first spacecraft went to Mars, they found nothing but dry, rocky plains.

Mercury

Mercury is 20 times smaller than the Earth. It is also three times closer to the Sun than we are. This makes its surface as hot as a gas fire. It is also covered in craters, so it looks a little like our Moon.

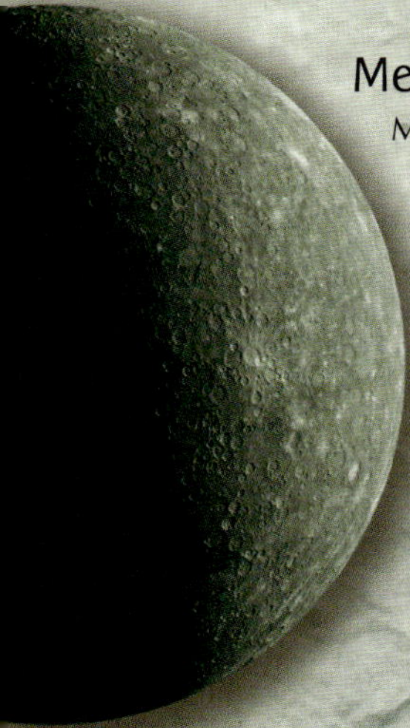

Mercury

Mars

Mars

Mars is about half the size of the Earth and covered in red soil, dust, and rocks. Its biggest mountain, Mount Olympus, is three times bigger than the highest mountain on Earth.

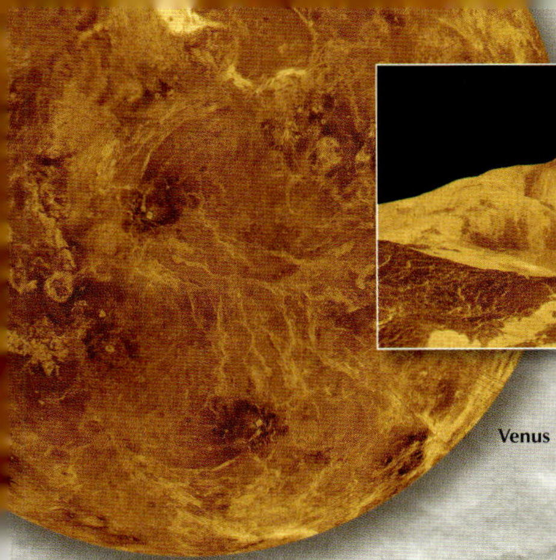
Venus

The Maat Mons volcano on Venus is five miles high.

Venus

Venus is only slightly smaller than the Earth and is covered in thick clouds of poisonous acid. Beneath these clouds the surface is hot and rocky.

Robots on Mars

Although nobody has ever been to Mars, lots of robots have. These machines, called rovers, have six wheels, and cameras for eyes. They can study rocks and soil, and do experiments.

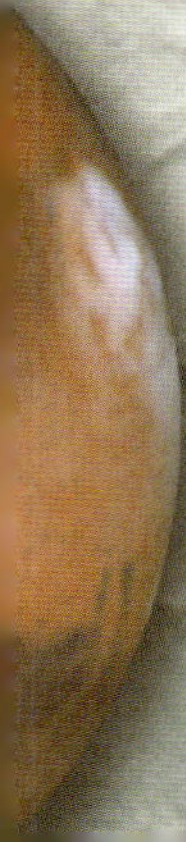

The gas planets

The gas planets are hundreds of times bigger than the Earth, and very different. A little like a snowball with a stone in its middle, each one of these planets is a huge ball of gas squashed together around a small rocky core.

Uranus

Uranus looks like a smooth blue-green ball. It is about four times wider than the Earth. It is different from all the other planets because it spins on its side. It also has some rings of dust and ice, like those of Saturn, only thinner.

Saturn

The second biggest planet is Saturn. It has beautiful shining rings. These are made of small bits of ice and dust. Saturn also has lots of moons. We know a lot about Saturn thanks to the exploratory spacecraft, or probe, *Cassini*, which began orbiting the planet in 2005.

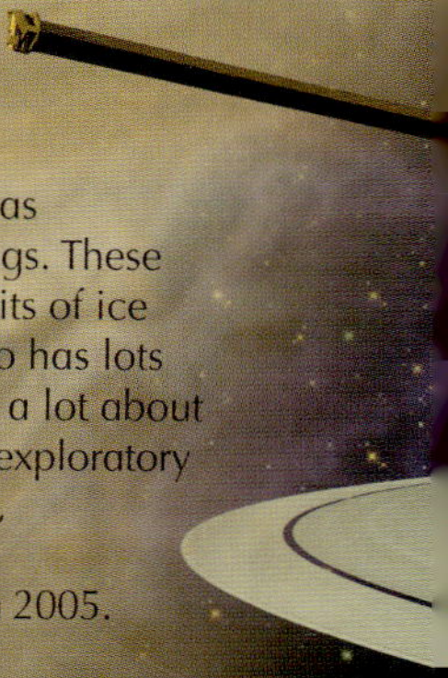

Jupiter

Jupiter is so big it could hold more than 1,000 Earths. It has a huge red circle on its surface called the Great Red Spot. This is actually a giant storm that is twice as wide as the Earth.

Neptune

Neptune is mainly dark blue, with a few darker spots and brighter clouds. It has the strongest winds of any planet. They blow four times faster than the winds on the Earth.

DID YOU KNOW?

Saturn has 62 moons. Its largest one, Titan, is the only moon in the solar system to have a thick atmosphere.

Dwarf planets and meteors

As well as the larger planets of the solar system, there are also a number of smaller worlds that astronomers call dwarf planets. These include Pluto and Eris.

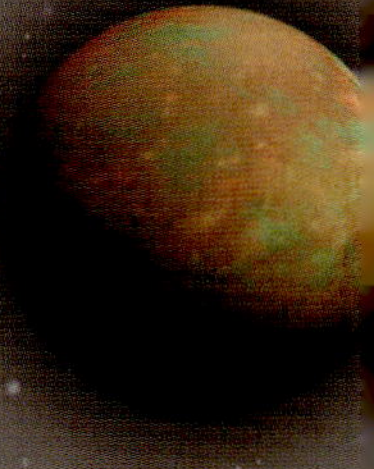

Pluto

Distant Pluto

Pluto is a small, cold planet right at the edge of the solar system. Its moon, Charon, is so big it is now thought to be a dwarf planet just like Pluto.

New Horizons probe

An *Atlas 5* rocket blasts off, carrying the *New Horizons* spacecraft.

New Horizons

In 2006 the *New Horizons* probe was sent to Pluto on a 10-year mission to find out more about this distant planet.

Meteorite

When a space rock hits the ground it is called a meteorite. The Hoba meteorite is the largest ever found. It is nearly 10 feet wide and weighs over 60 tons. It landed in Namibia, Africa.

Meteors

When tiny pieces of dust from comets hit the Earth's atmosphere, they get so hot they glow and burn up. Then they streak across the sky like fireworks, and are called meteors, or shooting stars.

Eris and Dysnomia

Slightly larger than Pluto, Eris is the latest planet to be discovered. It was only given its name in 2006. It has one large moon called Dysnomia.

Arizona crater

In Arizona, there is a huge bowl-shaped hole in the ground. It is 4,000 feet wide and 560 feet deep. It was made over 50,000 years ago, when a huge meteorite crashed into the ground.

Stars and galaxies

The nearest star to the Earth is the Sun. All the other stars look like tiny points of light because they are so far away. Many are actually much bigger than our Sun.

The life of a star

Although stars are just huge balls of burning gas, they are born, grow, and die just like living things.

Stars are born in huge clouds of gas that are called nebulae. Nebulae are sometimes called "star nurseries."

The star then burns steadily for about 10 billion years.

As the star begins to run out of gas, it expands to become a red giant.

Some red giants do not explode, but slowly shrink to become stars called white dwarfs.

Some red giants continue to expand and then explode. This is called a supernova. A supernova is the biggest explosion in our galaxy.

After a star explodes, the remains may shrink to almost nothing, forming a tight ball of gas. This has such enormous gravity that even light can't escape from it. It is now called a black hole.

How many stars?

Looking up at the night sky it seems as if there are millions of stars twinkling in the darkness. Nobody knows how many there really are. But without the help of a telescope, you can only see about 3,000.

Galaxies

Giant groups of stars are called galaxies. There are billions of galaxies in the universe, but our solar system is in a galaxy called the Milky Way.

Galaxies can be different shapes. This one is a spiral galaxy.

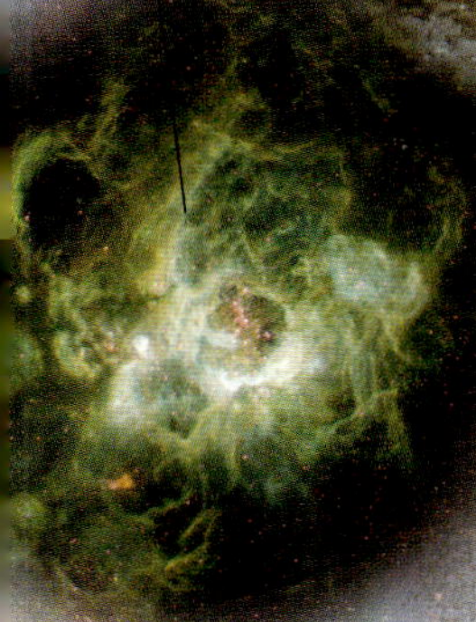

Nebula

Nebula

A nebula is a huge cloud of gas where stars begin to form. As the stars grow, the cloud begins to glow.

Seeing shapes in the stars

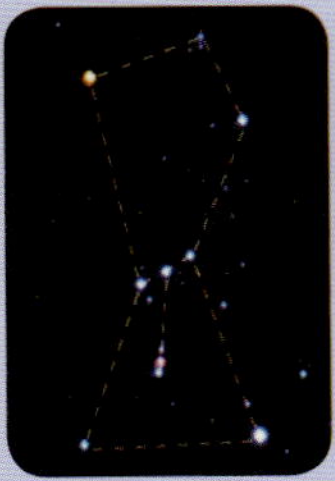

Orion the Hunter

The Great Bear, or Plow

When people first looked at the stars they made patterns out of them. We call these patterns constellations.

Telescopes

Galileo was the first person to study the night sky with a telescope. His telescope used lenses like those in a magnifying glass. It was very small. Today we study the sky with telescopes as big as houses.

DID YOU KNOW?

The biggest lens telescope in the world is at the Yerkes observatory in Wisconsin, USA. This telescope has a huge glass lens that is 3 feet wide.

Radio telescopes

Telescopes with lenses or mirrors capture light from distant stars. But stars also send out radio waves. So astronomers have built telescopes to pick up the signals. These radio telescopes are like huge satellite dishes. They need to be big because the signals are so weak.

Each one of these dishes is the size of a house.

Hubble

The Hubble telescope is a satellite that looks out into space. It takes pictures of stars and planets that are clearer than those we can take on Earth. This is because it does not have to look through all the dusty air that surrounds the Earth.

Refractor telescope

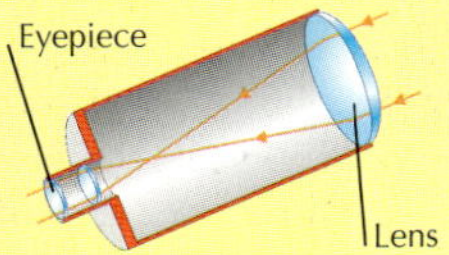

Reflector telescope

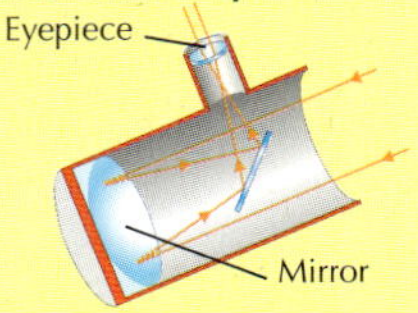

Telescopes

Telescopes that have a big lens at one end, just like an eye, are called refractors. Telescopes that use a big mirror, instead of a lens, are called reflectors.

Eyes on the sky

The world's biggest light telescopes use mirrors rather than lenses. This is because it is easier to make big mirrors than lenses. These huge telescopes are on Mount Haleakala in Maui, Hawaii. Telescopes are often built on mountains because the air is cleaner.

Blast off

Hundreds of people and a few animals have been into space. They all went there by rocket. Only rockets have the power to escape the Earth's gravity.

Launching a satellite

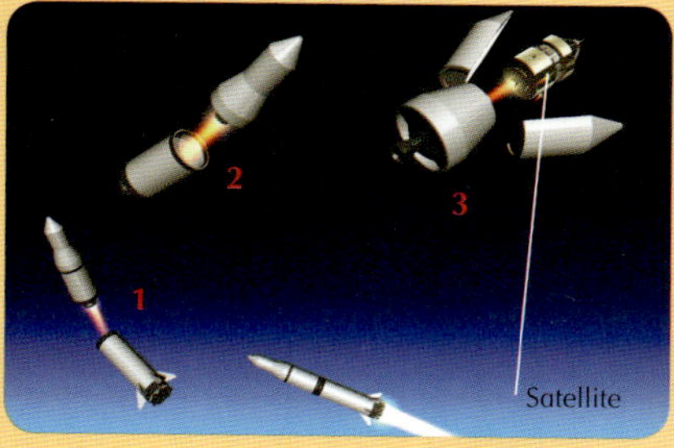

Rockets use a series of really powerful engines to blast them into space. When each engine has used up all its fuel, it falls back to the Earth. Some rockets have a big first-stage engine (1), a smaller second-stage engine (2), and a small booster engine (3).

Moon rocket

The most powerful rocket ever built was the *Saturn V*. Standing over 330 feet tall, this was the rocket that carried the *Apollo* astronauts to the Moon.

DID YOU KNOW?

The first person ever to go into space was the Russian Yuri Gagarin. He flew a *Vostok* rocket into orbit in 1961.

Weightless

In space there is very little gravity, so you become weightless and float around. Astronauts have to get used to this feeling so they can move safely. They practice in a special airplane that flies up high in the sky, and then dives to Earth very quickly.

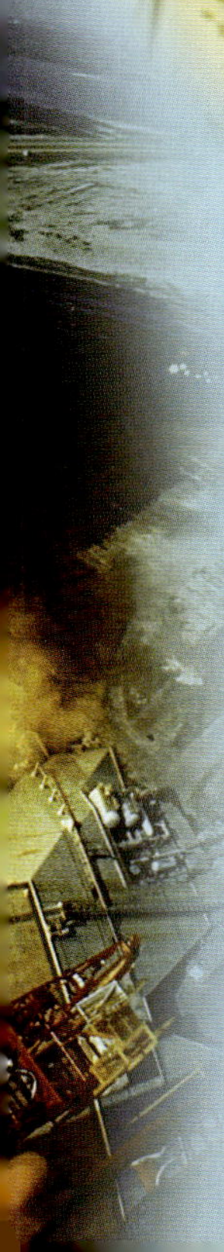

Splashdown

Some of the spacecraft that have returned to Earth have landed in the sea. This is the way the *Apollo* astronauts returned from the Moon. Parachutes help slow the spacecraft down, but it still lands with a big splash.

The space shuttle

The space shuttle is part rocket, part airplane. It can blast off into space and then fly back to the Earth.

The shuttle *Discovery* comes into land.

A shuttle space flight

The shuttle blasts off like a rocket (1). First its reusable boosters fall back to the Earth (2). Then its fuel tank drops away (3). The shuttle then usually spends up to 12 days in space (4) before gliding back to the Earth. As it flies through the Earth's atmosphere, it gets very hot (5). It lands on an extra long runway (6).

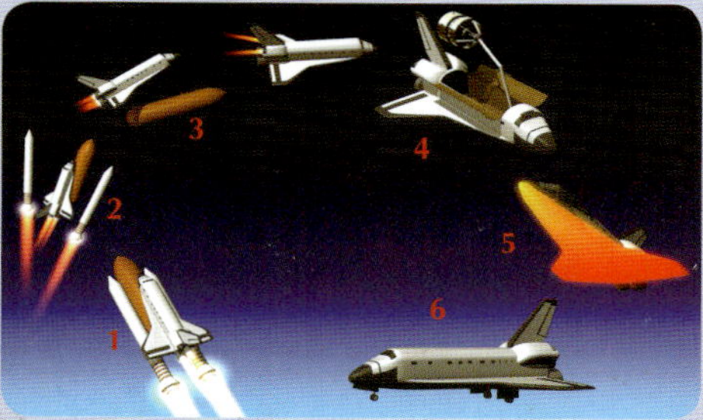

Back to Earth

Five space shuttles have been built and three are still in use. Each one carries a crew of five to seven astronauts. The shuttle is designed for around 100 launches.

Boosted into space

To break free of the Earth's gravity, the shuttle needs the help of two enormous solid fuel booster rockets. They return to Earth by parachute and can be reused.

Working in space

Once it is up in space, the shuttle opens the doors to its cargo bay. It can then unload its cargo, or catch broken satellites so the astronauts can mend them.

DID YOU KNOW?

The five space shuttles have all been named after famous ships. They are the *Columbia*, *Challenger*, *Discovery*, *Atlantis*, and *Endeavour*.

Space probes and satellites

Space probes and satellites are small spacecraft that have special jobs to do. Some visit distant planets and moons. Others send television programs or watch the weather.

Satellite launch

As the crane-like structures tip back, a Russian *Soyuz* rocket blasts off. This rocket is carrying the *GIOVE-A* satellite. Its job is to help people on Earth find their way around using special map computers.

Mars probe

Each space probe has a special job to do. This probe was sent to Mars in 2005. It is now circling the planet trying to find out if Mars ever had a lot of water like Earth. If it did, there may have been life on Mars.

Collecting samples

Launched in 2011, this Mars probe is part of a project to collect samples of Martian soil and bring them back to Earth. It will be the first time rocks from another planet have been brought back to Earth.

DID YOU KNOW? Satellites nearer the Earth fly faster. They can fly right around the planet in just 90 minutes. Satellites farther away can take a day or even longer.

This movable structure is used to service the rocket before blast-off.

Ozone hole

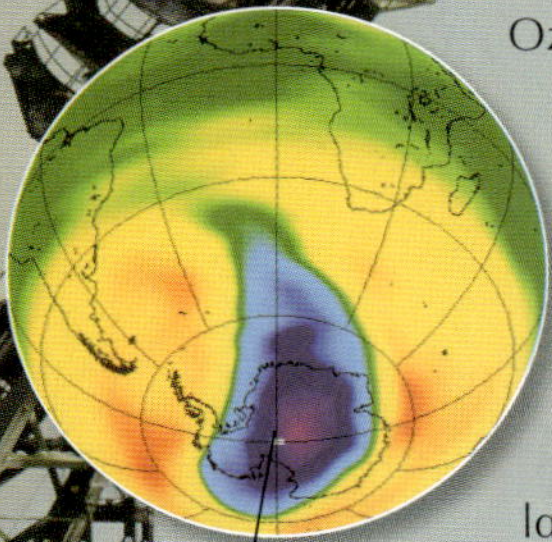

Ozone is gas found high in the Earth's atmosphere. It helps protect us from the harmful rays of the Sun. Recently, satellites spotted holes in the ozone layer above the poles. These have been caused by pollution.

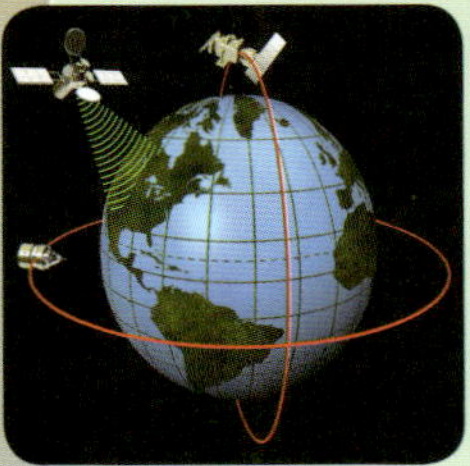

In orbit

There are about 3,000 satellites up in the sky above the Earth—although only about 1,000 are still working. Some are fixed in one position. Others circle the poles or the equator.

Going into space

Will you ever go into space? So far most of the people who have gone into space have been trained astronauts. But soon it might be possible to take a vacation there—if you have enough money.

SpaceShipOne

Launched from a special plane, called White Knight, SpaceShipOne blasted into space rather like the space shuttle. Soon tourists who want to see the stars could travel this way.

Exercise

In space you are weightless. This means your muscles don't work as hard. So astronauts try to keep fit by exercising.

Space suit

There is no air in space. It can also be either very cold or very hot. So astronauts must wear special space suits. These have their own air supply for the astronaut to breathe. They also help keep the astronaut at a comfortable temperature.

Space station

Space stations are like several big tubes joined together. People can live and work in them for many months. Many parts of the International Space Station, along with its crew, have been carried into space by the shuttle.

Some useful words

Aquatic
Describes a plant or animal that lives in water.

Asthma
An illness that makes breathing difficult.

Astronaut
A person who travels into space.

Astronomer
A person who studies the stars, planets, and space.

Ballast
Heavy material inside a hot-air balloon or submarine that helps it move up or down.

Battery
A portable supply of electricity.

Carnivore
An animal that eats other animals.

Concrete
A mixture of water, sand, stones, and cement that sets hard, like stone.

Conifer
An evergreen tree, such as a pine, that makes its seeds inside cones.

Crater
The mouth of a volcano, or a bowl-shaped hole caused by an explosion or something hitting the ground.

Crustacean
An animal without a backbone that has a body covered by an outer skeleton.

Deciduous
A tree that drops its leaves in fall, and then grows new ones in spring.

Desert
A sandy or rocky area where very little rain falls.

Empire
An area or number of countries that are controlled by one person or government.

Equator
An imaginary line that runs around the middle of the Earth.

Estuary
A place where a river meets the ocean and where saltwater mixes with fresh.

Evergreen
A plant that has green leaves all year.

Extinct
An animal or plant that once lived on the Earth but no longer exists.

Fossil
The remains of an animal or plant that have been buried for a very long time and become hard, like a stone.

Friction
The gripping force between two objects when they rub or slide past each other.

Fuel
Something that is burned to produce energy such as heat or power.

Gear
A toothed wheel that transmits, or carries, motion from one part of a machine to another.

Gills
The parts used by fish and some other aquatic animals to help them breathe underwater.

Global warming
The gradual increase in temperature of planet Earth caused by an increase in greenhouse gases.

Gravity
The force that pulls objects toward the Earth, or other planets and stars.

Greenhouse gas
A gas, such as carbon dioxide, that traps the Sun's heat, helping to make the Earth warmer.

Harvest
The time when farmers gather in ripened crops from the fields.

Herbivore
An animal that eats only plants.

Hull
The main part of a ship or boat that floats on the water.

Hurricane
A powerful storm with strong winds that often cause damage.

Krill
A small shrimp-like creature that forms the main food of some whales.

Lava
The hot, runny rock that comes out of volcanoes when they erupt.

Livestock
Farm animals, such as cows and sheep.

Metamorphosis
A big change in body shape that occurs when some animals, such as frogs and butterflies, change into their adult form.

Microscope
A tool with lenses that makes tiny objects look bigger so they are easier to see.

Mineral
A type of substance found in the ground, such as oil or coal. Also a substance needed in food to keep people healthy.

Nectar
A sweet, sugary liquid made by flowers.

Nocturnal
Describes an animal that is active at night.

Nutrient
A kind of food.

Omnivore
An animal that eats both plants and other animals.

Orbit
The circling path taken by something moving around a star, planet, or moon.

Ozone
A form of oxygen found high in the atmosphere. Ozone protects the Earth from the Sun's harmful rays.

Pharmacist
A person who is trained to prepare and sell medicines.

Plankton
The tiny plants and animals that are found in ponds, lakes, and oceans.

Polar
Describes the areas around the North and South Poles of the Earth.

Pollen
A fine powder produced by flowers so that they can make seeds.

Prey
An animal that is hunted by another animal for food.

Propeller
A screw with blades that spin round to drive a ship or aircraft.

Recycle
To use something again, such as old paper or glass bottles.

Reproduce
To produce young, or babies.

Resources
A supply of materials that is used to make the things we need.

Satellite
A moon or a spacecraft that is in orbit around the Earth or another planet.

Skeleton
The bony parts of a body that support the muscles and other soft parts.

Space probe
An unmanned spacecraft used for exploring, and which transmits, or sends, information back to Earth.

Streamlined
Describes something smooth and tapered that can move through water or air with very little effort.

Submarine
A special kind of boat that can travel underwater.

Tentacle
A long, feeler-like structure found on certain animals, such as anemones and squid.

Tornado
A violent storm with winds that whirl around very fast.

Tropics
Areas of the world that lie around the middle of the Earth, on either side of the equator. They are hot all year round.

Vacuum
A space that is completely empty, even of air.

Vapor
The steam or mist that is produced when some substances, such as water, are heated.

Vitamins
Various substances that are present in different food and which are essential to keep people healthy.

WEBLINKS

http://www.nhm.ac.uk/kids-only/index.html
http://www.un.org/Pubs/CyberSchoolBus/
http://www.countryreports.org/
http://www.pbs.org/wgbh/nova
http://www.exploratorium.edu
http://animal.discovery.com
http://www.earthlife.net
http://kids.nationalgeographic.com
http://guardians.net/egypt
http://www.factmonster.com
http://www.enchantedlearning.com
http://www.bbc.co.uk/schools/
http://www.nasa.gov/audience/forkids/
http://kids.earth.nasa.gov/
http://www.smithsonianeducation.org/students/

Index

T

U

V

W

X

Y

Acknowledgments

ARTWORK

David Lewis Illustration: 10BL Drew-Brook-Cormack, 12TL Drew-Brook-Cormack, 14BR Drew-Brook-Cormack, 21BL Drew-Brook-Cormack, 22TR Drew-Brook-Cormack, 26–27 BLBR Drew-Brook-Cormack, 29CL Drew-Brook-Cormack, 33CL Drew-Brook-Cormack, 40BL Drew-Brook-Cormack, 47TR Drew-Brook-Cormack, 49CR Drew-Brook-Cormack, 53BR Drew-Brook-Cormack, 55TR Drew-Brook-Cormack, 77T Simon Tegg, 81CL Peter Visscher, 88TR Drew-Brook-Cormack, 90B Drew-Brook-Cormack, 99B Drew-Brook-Cormack, 109TR Drew-Brook-Cormack, 115TR Bruce Hogarth, 117C,TL Bruce Hogarth, 118–119CRCL Bruce Hogarth, 121C Bruce Hogarth, 123TL Bruce Hogarth, 125CL Bruce Hogarth, 127CLCR Bruce Hogarth, 130TR Bruce Hogarth; **Precision Illustration:** 147CL Tim Loughhead, 149TL Tim Loughhead, 157CL Tim Loughhead, 159T Tim Loughhead, 161CL Tim Loughhead, 166BR Tim Loughhead, 169TL Tim Loughhead, 171TL Tim Loughhead, 173BC Tim Loughhead, 183TL Tim Loughhead, 185TL Tim Loughhead, 188BL Tim Loughhead, 197TR Tim Loughhead, 207CR Tim Loughhead, 208CL Tim Loughhead, 210BL Tim Loughhead, 213CR Tim Loughhead.

PHOTOGRAPHY

akg-images: 48BR Hervé Champollion; **Alvey & Towers:** 178BR; **Apple Computer:** 188TL; **BigStockPhoto:** 17CL Joao Freitas,87TR Giles DeCruyenaere, 87TL Giles DeCruyenaere, 90TL Giles DeCruyenaere, 92TL Giles DeCruyenaere, 94TL Giles DeCruyenaere, 94TR Razvan Photography, 95 aznatureAmon/Wilson Frisco, 96TL Giles DeCruyenaere, 98TL Giles DeCruyenaere, 100TL Giles DeCruyenaere, 102TL Giles DeCruyenaere, 104TL Giles DeCruyenaere, 106TL Giles DeCruyenaere, 108TL Giles DeCruyenaere, 110TL Giles DeCruyenaere, 156–157CRCL Paul Yates; **Bodyflight:** 187CLBodyflight Bedford/Ross Dagley Cleworth; **CLAAS:** 172–173CRCL; **Corbis:** cover C BloomImage, cover TR Liz Barry/Eye Ubiquitous, 1C Kennan Ward, 2–3C Stuart Westmorland, 4T Rob Howard, 8–9C Danny Lehman, 10TL Zefa/Jorma Jaemsen, 10–11TRTL Kennan Ward, 11C Zefa/Farhad Parsa, 13TR Steve Kaufman, 15BC Grant Smith, 16CL Saba/Shepard Sherbell, 17TR ANP/epa/Jasper Juinen, 17BR Maggie Hallahan, 20BL Archivo Iconografico, 24CR Stefan Meyers, 25CL epa/Miguel Vazquez, 25TR Zefa/Theo Allofs, 26CL James Randklev, 27T David Muench, 27CR Frans Lanting, 28TL Zefa/Guenter Rossenbach, 28BR Karl Weatherly, 29TR Owen Franken, 29BR Cordaiy Photo Library Ltd/Chris North, 31TL Stephen Frink, 32TR Reuters/Alexei Kalmykov, 32B Ecoscene/Sally A. Morgan, 33BR Reuters/China Newsphoto, 34–35C Adam Woolfitt, 36BR Jeffrey L. Rotman, 40TL Gian Berto Vanni, 41B Charles & Josette Lenars, 42–43TRTL Sygma/Sygma, 43BR Sergio Dorantes, 44L Kevin Fleming, 44–45TRTL Paul Almasy, 45CR epa/Paolo Aguilar, 46TL Barry Lewis, 46–47B Dave G. Houser, 47BR Earl & Nazima Kowall, 48B Reuters, 49T Zefa/Peter Adams, 49CL epa/Syed Jan Sabawoon, 49 BR San Francisco Chronicle/Paul Chinn, 52C Brian A. Vikander, 52BR Dale C. Spartas, 54C Milepost 92/W.A. Sharman, 54BL Louie Psihoyos, 55B Martyn Goddard, 56B Hulton-Deutsch CollectionHulton-Deutsch Collection, 57TR Sunset Boulevard, 57CR Reuters, 57BL Bettman, 58TR Casa Productions, 58BL Wendy Stone, 59TR Reuters, 59CL Mike Cassese, 59B Sygma/Les Stone, 60–61C Press-Telegram/Steven Georges, 63CL epa/Robin Utrecht, 63BR Peter Turnley, 65TR Michael Wray, 66TL David Turnley, 67CL Zefa/G. Baden, 68BR Stock Photos/Zefa/Lance Nelson, 69BR Louie Psihoyos, 71T Robert Harding World Imagery, 71BR Zuma/Art Stein, 74TL James Marshall, 74BR Wolfgang Kaehler, 75BR Liu Liqun, 77BR Sygma/Dung Vo Trung, 78TL Zefa/Stefan Schuetz, 78BL Zefa/Herbert Kehrer, 78TR Zefa/Alexander Hubrich, 79B Creasource, 80BR Kazuyoshi Nomachi, 81TR Reuters/Gaby Sommer, 81BR Robert Harding World Imagery/Christian Kober, 82TR Reuters/Reinhard Krause, 82BL Reuters/Brijesh Singh, 83T Sygma/Micheline Pelletier, 85CL Reuters/Seth Wenig, 85TR epa/Royal Household handout, 85BR epa/Narong Sangnak, 88B Tom Bean, 89CL Sygma/Bernard Annebicque, 89R Michael S. Yamashita, 91TL Gallo Images/Anthony Bannister, 92BC Hans Reinhard, 92–93TRTL Herbert Kehrer, 95TC Brandon D. Cole, 95C Jeffrey L. Rotman, 96–97BRBL Gary W Carter, 98–99TRTL Tim Davis/DLILLC, 100B Martin Harvey, 100–101TRTL Tim Davis/DLILLC, 101CL David A. Northcott, 101TR Kevin Schafer, 102B Gallo Images/Peter Lillie, 103BR Royalty-Free, 104TL Theo Allofs, 104BL Mary Ann McDonald, 105T Tom Brakefield, 105B David Stoecklein, 106BL Daniel J. Cox, 106–107TRCL Craig Tuttle, 107TR Zefa/Ute & Juergen Schimmelpfennig, 107BR Brandon D. Cole, 108B Peter Johnson, 110TL Francesc Muntada, 111T Ashley Cooper, 111B Gallo Images/Anthony Bannister, 112–113C George Shelley, 114TR Reuters, 114BR Rob Lewine, 115B Zefa/Joson, 116R Zefa/Matthias Kulka, 117BL Jim Craigmyle, 117TR Zefa/Gary Salter, 118BL Steve Prezant, 119R Reuters/Gary Hershorn, 120TR Roy Morsch, 120B Tom & Dee Ann McCarthy, 121TR Stephen Frink, 121BR epa/Marcos Delgado, 122CL dpa/Maurizio Gambarini, 124TL Zefa/Grace, 124BR Patrik Giardino, 125BR Laura Dwight, 126BL Zefa/Mika, 128TR Zefa/René Shenouda, 129CLReuters, 130BL Jim Erickson, 131TR Reuters, 131CL Reuters/Stringer, 132CR Zefa/Grace, 133TR Zefa/Stephen Beaudet, 133BL Zefa/Ole Graf, 133BR Zefa/G. Baden, 135TL Tom & Dee Ann McCarthy, 135CR Zefa/Ronnie Kaufman, 136CR Zefa/Robert Llewellyn, 136BL Ariel Skelley, 137TL Zefa/Jon Feingersh, 137CR Visuals Unlimited, 142C Larry Williams, 142BL Reuters/Reuters, 142–143BRBL epa/British Petroleum, 143TL Tom & Dee Ann McCarthy, 143R Visuals Unlimited, 144BL James Noble, 146C Rob Howard, 147B Zefa/Frans Lemmens, 149R Zefa/Klaus Hackenberg, 151R Jonathan Blair, 154BL George Hall, 155BR Tom & Dee Ann McCarthy, 156BL Onne van der Wal, 157TR Craig Aurness, 157BR Zefa/Matthias Kulka, 158L Paul A. Souders, 159B Natalie Fobes, 162BL Kevin Fleming, 162–163TRCL Paul A. Souders, 163BR Kevin Fleming, 167B Zefa/Ole Graf, 167TL Lester Lefkowitz, 167CR TWPhoto, 170T Royalty-Free, 170BR Reuters, 174TL Zefa/Erika Koch, 174BR Charles O'Rear, 178TL Reuters/Issei Kato, 179B Zefa/Kurt Amthor, 181BR Zefa/Klaus Hackenberg, 182BL epa/Armando Arorizo, 182–183CCL Handout/Reuters/Airbus Industrie, 185BR Handout/Reuters/Jack Atley, 186–187BRBL Robert Harding World Imagery/Christian Kober, 187TR Alan Schein Photography, 189BR Zefa/Michael A Keller, 193BR Roger Ressmeyer, 197CL Roger Ressmeyer, 197BR Alison Wright, 203TL Zefa/Hans Schmied, 203BC Charles & Josette Lenars, 205BC Roger Ressmeyer, 205BR Roger Ressmeyer, 206BC Roger Ressmeyer, 207 Roger Ressmeyer; **Dyson:** 168BL, 168TR; **European Space Agency:**199BC, 209T, 209BR, 212BR, 213BL, 213TR; **Getty Images:** 11BR First Light, 12CR The Image Bank/Eric Bean, 13CL Stone/David Hiser, 13BR Discovery Channel Images/Jeff Foott, 14CL Science Faction/Jim Sugar, 18CL The Image Bank/Pete Turner, 18–19TRTL The Image Bank/Steve Bronstein, 19B Reportage/Radhika Chalasani, 20TC Discovery Channel Images/Jeff Foott, 21CR National Geographic/Gordon Wiltsie, 22BC James Warwick, 23 Photographer's Choice/Frans Lemmens, 24BC Nordic Photos/Kalervo Ojutkangas, 25BL Stone/Greg Probst, 30–31BBL Photographer's Choice/Jeff Hunter, 31BR The Image Bank/Cousteau Society, 38CR The Bridgeman Art Library, 41TR Photodisc Green/Adam Crowley, 45B Taxi/Michael Freeman, 47TL Stone/Christopher Arnesen, 62TL Photonica/Jorg Greuel, 62BR Robert Harding World Imagery/Upperhall, 63TR Stone/Manfred Mehlig, 64L Stone/Nicholas Prior, 65CL Stone/Lawrence Migdale, 65BR ArabianEye, 66BR Getty Image News/Robert Nickelsberg, 67TR Taxi/Gary Buss, 67BR Stone/David Hanson, 68TL Stone/Terry Vine, 69TL Photodisc Green/Ryan McVay, 69TR Photographer's Choice/Ron Levine, 70TL Stone/Gary Yeowell, 70BR Stone/Tony Duffy, 72TL Stone/Chris Thomaidis, 73TL Photonica/PicturePress, 73CR The Image Bank/Luis Castaneda Inc, 75TL Reportage/Scott Nelson, 75TR Taxi/Rana Faure, 76BL Stone/Kevin Morris, 76–77TRTL Gulf Images/Pankaj & Insy Shah, 80TL First Light/Huy Lam, 83BR Asia Images/Steve Raymer, 84BL AFP/Lioel Healing, 84TR AFP/Kazuhiro Nogi, 86–87C Visuals Unlimited/Joe McDonald, 90TL Iconica/Andre Cezar, 91BR National Geographic/Joel Sartore, 96TL Photographer's Choice/Davies & Starr, 98BL Taxi/Peter Pinnock, 99TR Taxi/F. Millington, 102–103TRCL Image Bank/Riccardo Savi, 103TL Visuals Unlimited/Tom Ulrich, 108–109 BRCL Photodisc Green/Anup Shah, 109BR Winfried Wisniewski, 110BR Stone/David Hiser, 119C Image Bank/Terje Rakke, 122–123BRBL Taxi/Jim Cummins, 123TR Iconica/PM Images, 125TR Photodisc green/PNC, 128B Patrick Bernard, 129TR The Image Bank/Britt Erlanson, 131BR Stone/Don Smetzer, 132L The Image Bank/LWA, 134C First Light/Jim Craigmyle, 134BR Workbook Stock/Fontaine Su, 135BR Photodisc Green/David De Lossy, 137BL David De Lossy, 140TL Photodisc Green/Erin Hogan, 140BR Dorling Kindersley, 141TL The Image Bank/Pat LaCroix, 144C Photodisc Green/Robert Glusic, 145B Science Faction/Louie Psihoyos, 146BL Photodisc Green/Karl Weatherly, 148C Aurora/Jim Thornburg, 148–149BRBL Photonica/Henrik Sorensen, 150TR The Image Bank/Joseph Van Os, 150BL Workbook Stock/Bromberger-Hoover, 151BL Stone/Robert Frerck, 152TL Taxi/Photo & Co, 152BL Stone/David Davies, 152-153CRTL Stone/Doug Armand, 153CR Taxi/Tyler Stableford, 154C Photonica/Roberto Mettifogo, 158CR Stone/Michael Rosenfeld, 160TR Photodisc Green/Erin Hogan, 164–165C The Image Bank/Robert Holland, 166TL Taxi/Dana Neely, 171BR Taxi/Nick Dolding, 172BL Stone/Graeme Norways, 173TR Stone/Bruce Hands, 175TL The Image Bank/Yann Layma, 175CL Taxi/BC Moller, 175BR Stone/Lonnie Duka, 176BL Photodisc Blue, 177TR The Image Bank/Lester Lefkowitz, 177BL Photodisc Green/Jess Alford, 180C Taxi/Adastra, 180BL Photodisc Blue, 181TL Photonica/Jake Rajs, 183T Stone/Ross Harrison Koty, 183BL Taxi/Jeff Sherman, 184TL Photonica/VEER /Don Johnston, 184–185BRBL Stone/Martin Rogers, 185CR Iconica/Simon Plant; **iStockPhoto:** 6BL Bogdan Lazar, 6TL Charles Shapiro, 6–7RL Simon Moran, 7B Andrea Leone, 9TR Stasys Eidiejus, 10TL Stasys Eidiejus, 12TL Stasys Eidiejus, 14TL Stasys Eidiejus, 15TL Naphtalina, 16TL Stasys Eidiejus, 18TL Stasys Eidiejus, 20TL Stasys Eidiejus, 22TL Stasys Eidiejus, 23BL Jim Parkin, 24TL Stasys Eidiejus, 26TL Stasys Eidiejus, 28TL Stasys Eidiejus, 30TL Stasys Eidiejus, 32TL Stasys Eidiejus, 33TR Yanik Chauvin, 35TR WorldWideImages, 36TL WorldWideImages, 38TL WorldWideImages, 38–39BG Michael Valdez, 40TL WorldWideImages, 42TL WorldWideImages, 42BL Bogdan Lazar, 42CR Howard Sandler, 43BL Terry J Alcorn, 44BG Stephan Hoerold, 44TL WorldWideImages, 46TL WorldWideImages, 48TL WorldWideImages, 48L Robert Creigh, 48–49BG Amanda Rohde, 50TL WorldWideImages, 52BG Danny Warren, 52TL WorldWideImages, 53TR WorldWideImages, 54TL WorldWideImages, 56TL WorldWideImages, 56–57TRTL Bas Rabeling, 58TL WorldWideImages, 61TR GWFlash, 62TL GWFlash, 64TL GWFlash, 66TL GWFlash, 68TL GWFlash, 70TL GWFlash, 72TL GWFlash, 72–73BRBL JDWPhotos, 74TL GWFlash, 76TL GWFlash, 78TL GWFlash, 80TL GWFlash, 82TL GWFlash, 84TL GWFlash, 89BL Ruud de Man, 91CL Jenny Horne, 93TR Rick Hinson, 113TR Macroworld, 114TL Macroworld, 116TL Macroworld, 118TL Macroworld, 120TL Macroworld, 122TL Macroworld, 124TL Macroworld, 126TL Macroworld, 128TL Macroworld, 129CL José Luis Gutiérrez, 129C Tyler Olson, 130TL Macroworld, 132TL Macroworld, 134TL Macroworld, 136TL Macroworld, 138–139C Jerry McElroy, 141C Trina Denner, 145TR Charles Shapiro, 147TR Hogie Dale Hogan, 163TL Bebe Bailey, 165TR Alvaro Heinzen, 166TL Alvaro Heinzen, 168TL Alvaro Heinzen, 169CR Dan Brandenburg, 170TL Alvaro Heinzen, 172TL Alvaro Heinzen, 172TR TexasMary, 174TL Alvaro Heinzen, 176TL Alvaro Heinzen, 176TR BuzBuzzer, 178TL Alvaro Heinzen, 179TL Andrea Leone, 180TL Alvaro Heinzen, 182TL Alvaro Heinzen, 184TL Alvaro Heinzen, 186TL Alvaro Heinzen, 186L Simon Moran, 188TL Alvaro Heinzen; **L'Equip:**169BL; **NASA:** 5BR, 7R, 19TC, 155TR, 190–191, 191TR, 192TL, 192–193C, 194TL, 194–195C, 194–195C, 195TR, 196TL, 196BL, 196–197C, 198TL, 198CL, 198BR, 199TL, 199TR, 200TL, 200BL, 200TR, 201B, 201C, 202TL, 202L, 202C, 202CR, 203CR, 204TL, 204C, 204TR, 205C, 205CL, 206TL, 207TR, 208TL, 208R, 210TL, 210T, 211L, 211TR, 212TL, 212CR, 214TL, 214BL, 215TR, 214–215CRCL; **Naturepl:** 93BR Brian Lightfoot, 109TL Andrew Cooper, 127TR Hans Christoph Kappel; **Red Zebra Photo:** 49BL Gerald Peachey; **Scaled Composites LLC:** 214CL; **Science Photo Library:** 38BL Field Museum Chicago/Tom McHugh, 39CL Steve Gschmeissner, 39TR E. Hanumantha Rao, 39BR Tom McHugh, 94BL E.R Degginger, 97TC Gusto, 97CR Larry Miller, 122TR Alfred Pasieka, 126TR Adam Hart-Davis, 126TC Adam Hart-Davis, 141BR Eye of Science, 160C Jeremy Walker, 193TL David A Hardy/Courtesy PPARC, 203BL John Foster, **Scintilla Pictures:**114BL John Avon, 159C John Avon, 161TR John Avon, 161CR John Avon, 161BR John Avon; **Sony:**189TR; **Sony Ericsson:**188BC; **The LEGO Group:**189TL; **The Natural History Museum London:** 36TL Dinosaurs & Extinct Species/Paul D. Taylor and David N. Lewis, 36–37TRTL Dinosaurs & Extinct Species, 37BR Dinosaurs & Extinct Species/Michael Long.